EDWARD McWHINNEY is Professor of Law and Pol..... at Simon
Fraser University. He has been a constitutional adviser to both Canadian and
foreign governments and was the only English-speaking constitutional adviser to the Bertrand and Bourassa governments.

The Quiet Revolution and two major language bills have transformed
Quebec society. Ottawa's response to Quebec's constitutional demands has
been slow and erratic. Today Ottawa's bilingualism policies are under heavy
criticism. To complicate matters, the English-speaking provinces are seeking more autonomy; and the centralizing economics of John Maynard
Keynes – our modern 'father of Confederation' – are being challenged. Can
our constitution cope with these stresses? Should it be amended,
rewritten – or perhaps simply ignored?

Edward McWhinney offers the first thorough analysis of nearly two decades of constitutional development. His book examines Quebec's demands
since 1960 for social, economic, linguistic, and political self-determination,
and the implications of these demands for our federal system. It also looks at
the new pressures on such federal institutions as the Senate and the Supreme
Court coming from the constitutional proposals of the English-speaking premiers. The responses of successive federal governments, up to the Constitutional Amendment Bill of 1978, are studied.

Since the election in 1976 of a Quebec government officially committed to
separatism, the province has begun, without constitutional challenge, to
transfer power to a new social and economic élite. Edward McWhinney
scrutinizes the mechanisms of Quebec's transformation and, in his general
survey of constitutional evolution, suggests new possibilities for a truly 'cooperative federalism' and a 'renewed' Confederation.

Quebec and the Constitution 1960-1978

EDWARD McWHINNEY

UNIVERSITY OF TORONTO PRESS

Toronto Buffalo London

© University of Toronto Press 1979
Toronto Buffalo London
Printed in Canada
Reprinted 1979

Canadian Cataloguing in Publication Data

McWhinney, Edward, 1926–
    Quebec and the Constitution, 1960–1978
    Includes index.
    ISBN 0-8020-5456-0 bd. ISBN 0-8020-6364-0 pa.
    1. Canada-Constitutional history. 2. Quebec
    (Province) – History – Autonomy and independence
    movements. 3. Quebec (Province) – Politics and
    government – 1960–   I. Title.
    JL65.M39   320.9′71   c79-094224-0

Contents

Preface

This is a study of the Canadian federal constitution in the light of the 'Quiet Revolution' and the resulting French-Canadian aspirations for ethnic, cultural, and political self-determination. The English-Canadian question 'what does Quebec want?' – posed, for example, at Charlottetown in 1964 – brought irritated responses from French-speaking debaters who felt that the answers should be apparent to all parties. The simple political slogan, 'Maîtres chez nous!,' was not sufficiently concrete to be useful in actual intergovernmental relations; and this, I think, explains the preoccupation of younger French-Canadian intellectuals and professionals of the period with spelling out the institutional consequences of the Quiet Revolution and of national self-determination for French-Canadians.

The attention given in the present study to these essentially *a priori* academic formulations is explained by the special rôle that the intellectual occupies in Quebec political life in contrast with English-speaking Canada. Many of the university professors and lawyers engaged in the intellectual debate of the 1960s went on to become the political leaders of the 1970s; but their ideas also entered the domain of direct political action through the press and the media in general, which, again, have a special position in French Canada. These formulations, it is to be noted, were essentially in constitutional and legal terms, since that is the dominant mode of thought of the élite involved.

The chronology of the constitutional dialogue between French-speaking and English-speaking Canada since 1960 demonstrates a species of dialectical development. The English-speaking constitutional moves at the federal governmental level (and more rarely at the provincial level, as in the case of a courageous and innovative leader such as John Robarts of Ontario) tended to be reactive, somewhat delayed, and partial. At the same time, however, a significant new emphasis and direction emerged in the general French-English debate that was distinct and different from the constitutional formulation of the problem at the opening of the 1960s, namely the language question. If, of course, the problem is to be conceptualized in cultural and linguistic rather than constitutional terms, then the range of possible solutions may have to include also cultural and linguistic policy options as well as strictly constitutional and institutional remedies. Actually, the two different approaches to the problem and its definition are not necessarily mutually exclusive and may be complementary. From the time of the appointment of the federal government's Royal Commission on Bilingualism and Biculturalism, however, and certainly after the presentation of its final report, the cultural and linguistic approach was established as an 'alternative convention' to the definition and solution of the Quebec problem, and sometimes seems to have become dominant in both federal and provincial choices of community controls and remedies.

At the very time that the federal government was introducing distinctive (bilingual) federal language policies as its solution to what it saw as a growing crisis of national unity, the Quebec government ventured upon its own distinctive language policies, appointing a Royal Commission on the French Language and Language Rights in Quebec. A government response to a well-articulated cultural objective – the preservation of the embattled French language and culture in North America – ended with the Bourassa government's Bill 22 of 1974 and the Lévesque government's Bill 101 of 1977 as a virtual social and economic revolution. Language reform became the means of effecting the progressive transfer of economic decision-making in Quebec from an older Anglo-Saxon élite to the emerging new French-Canadian commercial élite.

By now, perhaps, some answers to the original question – 'what does Quebec want?' – may be clear. The problem is, in part at least, one of power – the degree and depth of participation in key social and economic decisions within Quebec by the overwhelmingly French-speaking majority. The problem may never really have been one of the constitution or of constitutional changes as such, these being no more than particular means for achieving a more effective sharing of social and economic power within Quebec. Substantive and timely constitutional and institutional changes would no doubt have helped to ameliorate the problem or to accelerate its solution, and they would still be useful in this regard even today. But the major changes within Quebec, since the Quiet Revolution and especially since the adoption of the two major language bills of the 1970s, have transformed Quebec society in a way that is, for all practical purposes, irreversible today. This transformation may permit a new calm and realistic approach to the present federal constitutional system and a recognition that this system is neither the cause of Quebec's problems nor an insuperable barrier to full cultural, social, economic, and political self-determination for French-Canadians within Confederation. No doubt the increasing awareness and acceptance of this fact within Quebec accounts in part for a certain, apparently conscious and deliberate de-emphasis of separatism as such in the Quebec government, and for a new emphasis on *association* rather than on *souveraineté* in the still conveniently abstract and undefined *souveraineté-association* formula. This same attitude may also explain the seeming willingness on the part of the Quebec government to profit from the opportunities presented by various non-Quebec events (such as the delay in calling a federal general election) for postponing the date of the referendum on separation promised by the *Parti québécois*.

Meanwhile, with the main Quebec protagonists – government and opposition – noticeably reluctant to date to put forward specific proposals for changing the constitution, English-Canada is delivering itself joyfully to the constitution-making game. Many of the current English-Canadian proposals seem like limited replies to Quebec proposals of yesterday – the reform packages of fifteen years ago. Is this an attempt to close the barn door after the horse has bolted? Will major constitutional changes be unnecessary if major social changes have already been achieved in Quebec by other means?

A special constitutional status for Quebec was proposed by Quebec intellectuals in the 1960s as an alternative to general Canadian decentralization. The latter they thought neither acceptable nor desirable for English Canada. If major constitutional changes are to come, would 'special status' do less damage to our federal system than some English-speaking premiers' proposals for a general reduction in federal decison-making and a substantial reduction in the powers of federal institutions? Some of these current provincial demands appear closer in sympathies and outlook to the constitutional theory of the Holy Roman Empire than to that of a genuinely federal state. In any case there have been, in Ottawa-Quebec relations since the 1976 Quebec election, elements of a pragmatic bilateral approach to issues as they arise. That is basically 'special status' without those elements of Cartesian *a priori* reasoning (derived from the French *droit civil*) which used to dismay English-speaking common-lawyers.

This study draws in part upon the written briefs submitted by the author at the invitation of the Task Force on National Unity (Pépin-Robarts Commission) and of the Special Joint Committee of the Senate and of the House of Commons on the Constitution of Canada. The balance of the study reflects several decades of writing and teaching on Canadian and foreign constitutional systems and the thinking and re-thinking which was part of that experience.

This book has been published with the assistance of the Canada Council, under its program of block grants to publishers, and of a grant from the Publications Fund of the University of Toronto Press.

E.McW.

Introduction

Since the surprise victory of the *Parti québécois* in November 1976, English-Canada and assorted political leaders and pundits have become preoccupied with constitutional law and with the drafting of a new constitutional charter to replace the British North America Act of 1867. One of my friends describes this new interest in constitution-making as the favourite English-Canadian 'cottage industry' of our times.[1] I prefer the metaphor of the cocktail party-game, since the supporting research and style of argumentation for these projects of constitutional innovation have been too often hurried and ephemeral. Some of the main actors in the game, such as Premier Lévesque (who is officially committed to separation), have been silent on the specifics of constitutional change. Others, like Prime Minister Trudeau, have seemed persuaded that the Quebec situation is not likely to be cured by constitutional change as such, and that the present constitution works reasonably well and needs at best only relatively modest, gradual change rather than a wholesale replacement.

Most observers feel the 1976 *Parti québécois* victory was not based upon separatism for that issue had been deliberately played down as a campaign issue by the Lévesque forces.[2] It was based rather on the record of the Bourassa government in countering high unemployment, its failure to deliver on election promises of a *fédéralisme rentable* and 100,000 new jobs for Quebec, and on the impact of the public hearings of the Cliche Commission on the role of organized crime in Quebec society and public life.

In addition, the Lévesque forces had formally committed themselves not to take Quebec out of the federal system without the prior authority of a majority vote in a referendum. They had also promised to hold that referendum during their time in office if victorious in the election. Given the passage of time since their victory, the referendum, if held, will probably be followed fairly shortly by a provincial election. Several fascinating scenarios arise from those two closely coincident events, and the political consequences in each case are dramatically different. Scenario one would involve victory of an unambiguous separatist proposal in the referendum, followed by re-election of the Lévesque government. Here the federal constitutional questions would presumably concern a Quebec withdrawal from Confederation, followed by institutional restructuring of a rump Canada without Quebec. Scenario two involves victory in the referendum for some deliberately modest proposal such as permission for the Quebec government to 'negotiate' with the federal government for separatism, 'souveraineté-association,' or some other formula. This would be followed by re-election of the Lévesque government. Here, the referendum mandate being ambiguous at best, the federal government might quite properly decide not to negotiate, and presumably Quebec's special claims would simply continue.

Scenario three sees clear defeat of a separatist proposal in the referendum, followed by re-election of the Lévesque government. This would no doubt see a politically chastened Lévesque government revert to the more traditional Quebec rôle of champion of special Quebec claims. Scenario four, defeat of a separatist proposal followed by defeat of the government, would undoubtedly mean a full-blooded revival of constitutional dialogue. Quebec intellectual leaders had tried unsuccessfully to initiate dialogue with English-Canada in the early and middle 1960s, at the high tide of the Quiet Revolution. We could therefore expect once more to hear argument, within the existing system over a 'special' constitutional status for Quebec within Confederation. This would be sought in order to maintan or protect the 'French fact' in Quebec and the claims of French-Canadians to full cultural self-determination within the Canadian federal system.

Looking back on the history of that abortive Quebec–English Canada constitutional dialogue of the 1960s one is reminded of the lesson of the Sibylline Books and of the merits of making political compromises while they are still timely. In this case, relatively modest changes in the BNA Act, to take account of Quebec's special interests, would have been timely and useful. However, such an approach would have been difficult to sell to English-speaking leaders in the 1960s, even if they had been predisposed to accept those changes.

English-Canada's constitutional thinking was shaped by an abstract conception of federalism in which all the provinces had to have a mathematically equal treatment under the constitution. Such a conception is not a general constitutional principle for federal systems. Nor is it completely true of Canadian federalism, which has equalization payments to correct regional disparities. There are even specific, positive law dispositions in the BNA Act which establish different provisions for various provinces, as to their representation in such federal institutions as the Senate.

Yet such arrangements are similar in their basic equity to the interpretation of equal protection under the law developed by the post-independence Supreme Court of India. One should treat equal things equally but may constitutionally apply different treatment for persons or institutions operating under special conditions or disabilities. It would undoubtedly have been asking too much of English-speaking leaders of the 1960s to accept a 'special constitutional status' for Quebec. They might have been induced by a rather more subtle Quebec approach to concede some particularized constitutional arrangements for Quebec in certain situations. However, the Pearson government elected in 1963 was committed almost immediately to its own Royal Commission on Bilingualism and Biculturalism (the Laurendeau-Dunton Commission). It would have been bad constitutional etiquette and perhaps premature for the Pearson government to propose its own constitutional solutions before the royal commission terminated its mandate. The commission's work was finally completed by the end of the 1960s. It saw Quebec and Canada's dilemma – and possible answers – in essentially linguistic terms. It is known that the commission had planned a special volume of its final report on constitutional implications of bilingualism. Constitutional rather than linguistic recommendations would have been the keystone of its proposals.

The personality of the francophone co-chairman of the commission, André Laurendeau, was crucial for the achievement of a consensus on constitutional change in a commission where the non-francophone members out-numbered the francophones. The commission was strongly divided in its preliminary discussions on policy recommendations in the proposed constitutional volume. André Laurendeau's sudden death in mid-1968 abruptly ended all hope of a workable compromise within the commission and led to the shelving of the proposed constitutional volume. In the end, the commission's emphasis, *faute de mieux*, was predominantly linguistic, and the solution advanced was also linguistic.

The Trudeau government which had succeeded Pearson responded correctly and in accordance with protocol by adopting the commission's recommendations and applying a linguistic solution. A linguistic rather than a constitutional approach became the prime federal policy. Federal initiatives in the constitutional field, such as the proposals for the so-called Victoria Charter of 1971, were directed to technical issues such as the 'patriation' of the BNA Act as a Canadian statute or the development of new constitutional amending machinery. They did not really address the fundamental Quebec claims of the 1960s.

One major consequence of Laurendeau's premature death and of the 'missing volume' of the commission's final report was the absence of a substantive debate between Quebec and English Canada on the constitution in the sixties and early seventies. Positions, however, soon polarized, and intermediate options, such as 'special constitutional status,' involving changes *within* Confederation, were replaced by the separatist option. A constitutional debate would have demonstrated the relation, if any, between the language and the constitutional issues; the extent to which the language problem was purely linguistic or something more; and, finally, the comprehensiveness or otherwise of a federal solution framed in strictly linguistic terms. The constitutional approach was finally invoked in a substantial way by English-speaking provincial leaders and the federal government after the 1976 Quebec election. Those political leaders in Quebec who had favoured the intermediate options and who had some political mandate for them were now in eclipse, and a dialogue over constitutional change within Confederation was now hardly possible between Quebec and Ottawa. There remains then the question of the general utility of large-scale debate in English Canada on fundamental change to the existing federal system, and the BNA Act in particular, before a new Quebec consensus emerges. Proposals for constitutional change emanating from English-speaking Canada undoubtedly contribute in some way to the internal Quebec debate. But it is difficult to advance proposals conditional upon whichever one of the radically different political scenarios should develop in Quebec over the crucial next several years. If the proposals for change are intended to be firm, they must be ones that the rest of Canada is prepared to live with happily even if Quebec decides to leave Confederation. Therefore, current proposals from provincial leaders need to be appraised on their merits as constitutional reforms in their own right, regardless of the special Quebec element. Senator Eugene Forsey's satirical appraisal in his appearance before the federal Task Force on National Unity (Pépin-Robarts Commission) is scarcely exaggerated:

Some months ago, a friend said to me: 'There is a strong wind blowing for constitutional change.' I replied 'Yes. And "wind" is exactly the word to describe most of it. Many of those who talk about a new or revised Constitution haven't the vaguest notion of what they would put into it; others have very clear notions, but they are completely crazy.'[3]

If the time is not ripe for comprehensive constitution-making, it may still be useful for the federal government to move, if only to show its ability to accept constitutional change where demonstrably necessary and also to maintain control of the initiative in such matters. A likely area for any such federal initiative would be in areas of general constitutional significance not limited to federal or federal-provincial matters. The development of more adequate administrative and legal controls upon executive power and proliferating bureaucracy and the constitutional redefinition of the relations between man and the state in the post-industrial society both seem especially favourable issues. Constitutional reform need not be limited to federal problems, which are not even necessarily the most important problems of post-industrial society in Canada.

Within the range of strictly federal problems there is of course in the BNA Act, as in most working constitutional charters, a certain amount of 'give,' or built-in flexibility. This permits continuing adaptation of the original written text to new societal interests and demands. This open quality of the BNA Act facilitates pragmatic accommodation – in particular issues of federal-provincial relations. The federal government should maximize the possibilities for such accommodation. It has a certain flexibility with the timing and staging of constitutional change, once it is committed to change as such. It does not need to act on everything at once but can determine its own priorities and proceed on a step-by-step basis. It has also had, since the passage of the BNA Act (No. 2) in 1949, the power of unilateral initiative in areas wholly within the legislative competence of the federal government, particularly on such federal institutions as the Senate and the Supreme Court.

The emphasis on unilateral federal initiatives on matters *wholly* within federal legislative competence draws attention to marginal questions, such as provincial representation in the Senate, specified in section 22 of the BNA Act, as amended. These are of 'mixed' (federal *and* provincial) concern, even though the institutions concerned are federal. These marginal questions may therefore be incapable of amendment by the federal government acting alone. On the Senate, the federal Government acted on a request made by a majority vote of the Senate-House Special Joint Committee on the Constitution, and in November 1978 referred the issue to the Supreme Court for Advisory Opinion on constitutional aspects. The Advisory Opinion reference is limited to the Senate. Beyond such marginal questions, however, unilateral federal initiatives to amend the constitution under the BNA Act (No. 2) 1949 – now section 91(1) of the BNA Act – raise purely political, not constitutional and legal, considerations.

If the federal government feels the time is ripe it should not hesitate to act in these areas without delaying indefinitely for recalcitrant provincial governments. The 'politic of mutual example' in international relations is posited upon a constructive unilateral gesture by one party in the hope that other parties may be induced, by the example, to move in a similar spirit. Thus pragmatic methods may contribute to the continuing constitutional change that has characterized our system since its inception in 1867.

QUEBEC AND THE CONSTITUTION 1960-1978

1
Constitutions in Flux

A constitutional system is normally thought of as a constitutional charter or a similar single text or document. Not all countries, however, have reduced their constitutional law to written form. Even where this has been done, the constitutional law may not be contained in any one basic text. There may be instead a collection of constitutional texts, or even a more informal constitutional repertory. Perhaps several written texts will be included, along with a number of informal practices or 'glosses' added by executive practice (constitutional custom or convention) and authoritative interpretation, whether judicial or otherwise.

It is a truism of comparative law that some simple, beautifully written constitutional charters remain poetic exercises – nominal, and not normative. Some of the more untidy constitutional systems – dispersed over many legislative texts and digests of official practice – are genuinely operational. The distinction between constitutional 'law-in-books' and constitutional 'law-in-action' is a basic one. The constitution-making game becomes easy and pleasant – an abstract, academic play with coloured balloons – if one takes no responsibility for the application and implementation of one's proposals. It was said of the drafters of the Weimar Constitution of Germany in 1919 – a brilliantly intellectual, 'professorial' document – that they had elaborated a philosophers' charter, and that their only problem was to find a people worthy to live with it.

Constitutional systems that have evolved since the American constitution of 1787 – the first and ultimate exercise in rationalized constitutionalism – generally undertake to set out in one basic charter the key governmental institutions and their decision-making processes. They may also attempt some definition of the fundamental values or purposes of the society for which the charter has been created. This may be done in a constitutional preamble, or in a constitutional Bill of Rights (and the related 'Directive Principles of State Policy' that were so popular with constitution-drafters of the 1930s and the 1940s).

There are some dangers in introducing such elaborations of political, social, or economic principle directly into a constitutional charter. Public tastes tend to change, and statements of philosophical principle ventured upon too categorically may simply reflect the whims of a particular era. The fate of the constitutional system itself may become bound up with the survival of the values of an era long gone. On the whole, if such assertions of faith must be inserted into the charter, it seems better to keep them general rather than specific, allowing a continually changing interpretation as the society itself changes. And it would certainly seem better to limit them to issues of political principle – political rights – and to eschew definitions of social and economic policy where the fluctuations in community expectations and demands are likely to be most sweeping and most rapid.

Another key aspect of a constitutional system is that it rests – and must rest, if it is to be and remain workable – upon certain political presuppositions. Fundamental societal compromises must precede and accompany the act of constituent power involved in the enactment of a constitutional charter and the setting up of the constitutional system itself. This is another demonstration of the symbiotic relation between law and society. In technical terms, these fundamental compromises constitute a pre-legal, *meta*-legal basis – the constitutional *Grundnorm* as Kelsen called it, the necessary starting-point for a constitutional system.

For a new federal constitutional system, the decision to federate in the first place constitutes the *prior* constitutional act. This decision can be made on a free, consensual basis, or imposed by the prevailing élite, whether imperial or other. In an already existing federal system, the decision whether to continue the federation or to allow the constituent peoples to go their separate ways is also an extra-legal question. It will be determined on political rather than strictly legal grounds, even if the existing system has made an advance ruling upon the constitutionality of such a breakaway. The task of government decision-makers in such cases is to maximize the advantages – political, social, and economic – of maintaining the existing system. If the original societal compromise, whether consensual or imposed, has weakened or disappeared, it must be replaced by a new, genuinely inclusive one. Such a task is, however, political and not legal, even if its successful accomplishment is a prerequisite to the maintenance of a working constitutional system.

When we speak of an *old* federalism, we are speaking of the classic Anglo-Saxon federal systems[1] represented by the United States. We also include those surprisingly imaginative experiments in devolution and decolonization, the federal or quasi-federal entities established by the British government. These examples include certainly Canada and Australia; possibly South Africa; and less probably the Dyarchy and other constitutional elaborations for the Indian sub-continent.

These systems are ventures in rationalized constitutionalism – attempts to render, in institutionalized, charter form, the fundamental political accommodations and compromises that had preceded them. They are products essentially of liberal enlightenment – in the case of the British Empire, of paternal liberalism, albeit often surprisingly generous. But their utility, as constitutional forms, depended upon either the maintenance of those fundamental compromises that had preceded their adoption or the replacement of the original compromises by new and equally effective ones.

This process of continuing and self-renewing consensus, notwithstanding the dramatic societal transformations during the same period, can be observed in the case of the US federal constitution. In spite of recurring political and economic crises, the federal system has succeeded in retaining its original vigour, with the original federal institutions of 1787 progressively and creatively adapting to new demands and pressures. The same process can be observed within the Australian federal constitution, though the task was easier there because of the basic homogeneity of race, language, culture, and political expectations.

The process is not apparent in the case of the other classic British Empire – derived federal systems where the original consensus has either not been maintained or not been successfully replaced by a new one. Imperial India fissured in the wake of decolonization, creating political and territorial divisions on the sub-continent that have not yet been finally determined. South Africa proved itself incapable of successfully resolving the more immediate political problem of European bi-nationalism. Nor could it cope with the long-range and far more complex challenge of building a workable multiracial political system in which the two European élites would themselves constitute a small minority. Successive crises have also attended the British ventures in federalism and devolution in Ireland, Malaysia, Rhodesia, the West Indies, and Cyprus, to name only the more notable examples.

Canada, as we know, is experiencing substantial difficulties in accommodating the drives for national self-determination for French-Canadians. The devolution or decentralizing of governmental decision-making in cultural, social, and economic spheres would necessarily be involved.

Most of the accepted truths almost axioms – about federalism and federal systems are generated from the few successful federal states originally governed by the British. Is there a general and inevitable trend to centralization of decision-making power in federal systems? Is federalism simply a transitory step on the way to governmental unity, as Bryce foresaw? These are propositions induced too sweepingly from the experience of the United States, Canada, and Australia. Two world wars and the Great Depression accentuated centripetal federal forces as a means of facilitating central planning and decision-making in those countries.

Dicey's criticism of the legalism, conservatism, and governmental weakness inherent in federalism reflected both his academic training and the intellectual predilections of a man wholly accustomed to a centralized, unitary system of government.[2] Dicey signally failed to comprehend the institutional sophistication involved in governing a multi-national society on the basis of juridical equality of constituent units rather than of hierarchical superiority as in the British Empire. Dicey could neither understand nor sympathize with Roman Catholic claims to participation in the government of Ireland.[3]

Most propositions about federalism refer to the Anglo-Saxon models. They do not take account of the experience of those multi-lingual, multi-national systems of continental Europe. In the end these often failed, but because of the complexity of the political problems involved rather than failure of the sophisticated institutions developed for them. The Austro-Hungarian dual monarchy of 1867, in spite of all its defects, did hold together for half a century until the military downfall. The Danubian confederation to which it probably could have (with imagination) given way remained a dream of the élite. The post-1918 'Succession' states were too small to resist an intransigent neighbour like Nazi Germany.

The trend in Europe since the Second World War is once more towards federalism and regionalism. This is so even in those countries now joined or joining in supra-national political and economic integration. What is striking is the coexistence of *centripetal* and *centrifugal* trends in all the major Western European countries, whether plural or unitary in form and structure. Decentralization, the key word within the existing nation-state, involves formation of local governments or assemblies and devolution of decision-making on a regional basis.

France, for example, as Giscard d'Estaing claims, is rediscovering the virtues of a cultural diversity lost when Richelieu put down the powerful provincial nobles in the cause of a strong, centralized nation-state. Belgium is moving from a plural and institutional to a more genuinely federal system. Britain is beginning to cede power, however reluctantly, to local assemblies in Wales and Scotland. Regional autonomist or separatist groups, based on cultural and linguistic ties that transcend political frontiers, are threatening the internal stability of a number of Western European states – all this at a time of unprecedented harmony and coordination in fiscal, economic, and foreign policy, and when the supra-national institutions for effectuating those common policies are growing apace.

The new supra-national federalism and the recognition of national particularism within the existing nation-state constitute perhaps the most interesting and enriching developments in post-war constitutionalism.[4] They are of course the obverse of the chauvinistic emphasis of the pre-war years on *autarchy* and on homogeneity within the nation-state. This attitude is what is meant by the new pluralism, and it remains as yet a largely continental European, civil law development that has yet to penetrate the Anglo-Saxon world.

The political problem within Canadian federalism has been evident, for those who could read the signs, ever since the inauguration of the Quiet Revolution in Quebec in the early 1960s. It has simply been brought out into the open by the electoral victory of the *Parti québécois* in the 1976 election. The election of the Lévesque government has produced a spate of public debate and related activity in English Canada, all ostensibly devoted to the cause of a new federalism in Canada. This, ideally, should contain French-Canadian drives for self-determination within a continuing federal structure for Canada. Large public conferences have been organized in English Canada – in Toronto and in Banff, financed directly and indirectly or otherwise actively patronized by English-speaking political leaders. Their aim seems to have been the creation of a vastly more decentralized federalism than heretofore, with substantial shifts in law-making powers to the provincial governments at the expense of the central government. Further changes of a 'federalizing' character, designed to promote effective provincial or 'regional' participation in existing central institutions such as the Senate and the Supreme Court, have also been advanced.

Two general comments seem proper, at this stage, in regard to all this English-Canadian political activity on behalf of a new federalism. Public enthusiasm for constitutional change is sufficiently rare for it to be welcome without any thought of the political motives or ambitions of its main sponsors. Yet it would be rather more persuasive today if the main English-speaking protagonists of constitutional change, whether political or academic, had shown earlier interest in major reform of the federal structure.

Again, all this latter-day English-Canadian political activity may simply serve to vindicate the lesson of the Sibylline Books already referred to on the utility of offering and accepting political compromises while they are still timely and relevant. There was a time in the 1960s when still determinedly federalist French-Canadian political leaders were pressing for a restructuring and decentralizing of the Canadian federal system *vis-à-vis* Quebec. This was identified as special or particular constitutional status for Quebec within Canadian federalism, or even so-called *associate state* status which was still conceived of and presented as a constitutional arrangement within Confederation.

These Quebec proposals were not accepted by English-Canadian leaders, whether provincial or federal; and they found no support at all within the English-Canadian academic community. By the irony of history English-Canadian political leaders now show themselves, a decade or more later, prepared to accept large elements of the earlier Quebec proposals. A more decentralized federal system is sought through applying these proposals as a general plan affecting all the provinces equally, and not simply Quebec on a particularist basis. Quebec attitudes, however, have now evolved beyond the special claims of the 1960s. The point has perhaps been reached where compromise between Quebec and English Canada on the basis of Quebec's earlier claims is no longer possible. As the American legal realist leader, Judge Jerome Frank, used to say: 'That was then and this is now!'

2
Canada's Changing Constitution

A constitution inevitably tends to change as the society for which it was intended changes. A constitution that did not change would, by definition, be nominal and not normative – an exercise in logic and not in life. Constitutional change is normally thought of as occurring through formal amending machinery inserted directly into the constitutional charter itself. Not all constitutions, however, have such provisions in their constitutional charter, and even where they do it may not be the only or the principal agency of change.

Constitutions can and do change through developing governmental practice, and so ripen in time through more or less binding constitutional precedent – what is known in British constitutional theory as the emergence of a constitutional custom, or convention of the constitution. But constitutions may also be modified and even transformed altogether through judicial interpretation. A final appellate tribunal may have authority to review the constitutionality of laws adopted by the legislatures or of the executive application of those laws – judicial review of the constitution.[1] In the United States no formal provision for judicial control of constitutionality was inserted in the charter itself. However the Supreme Court has successfully asserted such a rôle since Chief Justice John Marshall's seminal opinion in *Marbury* v. *Madison* at the beginning of the nineteenth century.[2] Other, more recent constitutional systems – like those of post-war West Germany and Japan – have been strongly influenced by the successful American model.

In Canada, judicial review of constitutionality stemmed directly from the subordinate character of the British North America Act of 1867. The Imperial Privy Council, the highest appellate tribunal of the British Empire, exercized control over the conformity with Imperial law of the enactments and executive practice of the colonial legislatures, including of course those of Canada. Canada evolved into a fully independent, self-governing country by the 1930s. Judicial review of the BNA Act had been exercised so continuously and so effectively by the Privy Council that the imperial roots of judicial review had been entirely forgotten and it had entered into the status of a constitutional practice – convention of the constitution – in its own right.

With the final abolition of appeals from Canadian courts to the Imperial Privy Council in 1949, the Canadian Supreme Court began to exercise judicial review of the constitution, just as the Privy Council had done before it. There were no second thoughts as to the constitutional legitimacy of the practice. In fact judicial review of the constitution has been the principal instrument of change for the Canadian constitution since 1867. There were pendulum-like swings in judicial interpretation of the BNA Act during that period, depending upon the dominant judicial personalities involved and their philosophies of constitutional interpretation, and of federalism and of government generally. The dominant rôle of judicial review in Canadian constitutional law-in-action has not changed significantly since the 1949 emergence of the Canadian Supreme Court as final appellate tribunal in its own right.

In its preamble, the constitution of Canada speaks of the desire of the provinces of Canada to be 'federally united into one Dominion under the Crown of the United Kingdom of Great Britain and Ireland, with a Constitution similar in principle to that of the United Kingdom.' Historically, then, the constitution of Canada, like the constitution of the United States, stems from the union of a number of existing units. The provinces of Lower Canada (Quebec), Upper Canada (Ontario), Nova Scotia, and New Brunswick joined together in 1867 to form the new Dominion of Canada. The remaining six provinces have joined Canada since that time.

In formal juridical terms, the fundamental instrument in which the Canadian constitution is embodied – the British North America Act of 1867 – is a statute of the United Kingdom Parliament.[3] Thus, though Canada in 1867 became a self-governing Dominion within the British Empire by virtue of the act, her international status for many purposes was still something less than that of a full sovereign state. In 1931, the conventions governing the relationship of the United Kingdom to the self-governing dominions were crystallized in the Statute of Westminster. However, a few vestiges of Canada's former legally subordinate position still remained.

First, the BNA Act contains no provision as to its own amendment. Constitutional change in Canada had perforce to be achieved by recourse to the original legal source of the Canadian constitution, the United Kingdom Parliament. The considerable number of amendments since 1867 have been in the form of acts of the United Kingdom Parliament. Today, all political parties are satisfied as to the desirability of some amending procedure that can be operated by the Canadian people themselves. Yet it seems agreed that the exact formula for amendment, a matter of some considerable controversy as yet, must finally be embodied in an act of the United Kingdom Parliament in order to become effective.

Second, until 1949 an appeal existed from the Canadian Supreme Court to the Imperial Privy Council. The rôle that the Privy Council actually played in exercising ultimate judicial review of the Canadian constitution is one of the more controversial aspects in Canada's post-1867 constitutional history.

The Canadian constitution was probably designed, as English-Canadian academics have usually contended, to provide a highly centralized government. There was a reaction to the then recent US Civil War and a response to the lessons supposedly to be derived thence of the dangers of too decentralized a federal system. What made the new system reconcilable with the political reality of British North America at that time was that law and society operated together in more or less symbiotic relation.

The positive law of the supposedly centralizing BNA Act followed upon fundamental political accommodations and compromises. These went back to the military Capitulations of 1759, the Treaty of Paris of 1763, and the Quebec Act of 1774, and later, related, organic arrangements between French and English. They involved acceptance of the privileged status within Quebec of the Roman Catholic church and its dependent institutions and practices, and of the French *droit civil*.

The tolerant civic pluralism of British imperialism in the late eighteenth century had facilitated French Canada's acceptance of the conquest of 1759. This pluralism made it possible for French Canada to resist the blandishments offered by the Americans in 1776, and again during the War of 1812. Maintenance of these fundamental political compromises between French and English constituted an essential *pre-* or *meta*-legal assumption of the British North America Act of 1867. It represented the constitutional *Grundnorm*, the basic premise or political and societal starting-point of the post-1867 constitutional system. Maintenance of that original *Grundnorm* or its replacement by some new consensus would thereafter be a pre-condition for the survival of the Canadian nation.

The drafters of the Canadian constitution clearly intended the federal Parliament's legislative powers to be of paramount importance. The system of government under the BNA Act was to be a centralized federalism.[4] The

BNA Act established a distribution of legislative authority between the two types of governing authority. Unlike the US constitution, no legislative powers were denied to both federal and provincial governments – there is no Canadian bill of rights. As the Lord Chancellor, Lord Loreburn, said, 'there can be no doubt that under this organic instrument the powers distributed between the Dominion on the one hand and the provinces on the other hand cover the whole area of self-government within ... Canada. It would be subversive of the entire scheme and policy of the Act to assume that any point of internal self-government was withheld from Canada.'[5]

Under section 91 of the BNA Act the federal government is given a general power to make laws for the 'Peace, Order, and good Government of Canada, in relation to all Matters not coming within the Classes of Subjects by this Act assigned exclusively to the Legislatures of the Provinces.' Section 91 goes on to declare that 'for greater Certainty, but not so as to restrict the Generality of the foregoing Terms,' the legislative authority of the federal Parliament shall extend to all matters coming within a list of twenty-nine enumerated subjects. Under section 92, the provincial legislatures are given exclusive legislative authority over a list of sixteen subjects, of which perhaps the two most interesting from the constitutional viewpoint have been section 92(13), 'Property and Civil Rights in the Province,' and section 92(16), 'Generally all Matters of a merely local or private Nature in the Province.'

It also seems clear that the general federal power to make laws for the 'Peace, Order, and good Government of Canada' was intended to be the major source of federal legislative power. The twenty-nine specific heads of federal legislative power enumerated in section 91 were merely illustrations of the general power. As Dean Kennedy said:

The federal powers are wholly residuary for the simple reason that the provincial powers are exclusive; and the twenty-nine 'enumerations' in Section 91 cannot add to the residue; they cannot take away from it ... They have no meaning except as examples of the residuary power, which must be as exclusive as is the grant of legislative powers to the provinces. The enumerated examples of the residuary power cannot occupy any special place; they cannot be exalted at the expense of the residuary power, for that would 'restrict the generality' of that power. It all looks reasonably simple, and Sir John A. MacDonald was perhaps justified as he looked at the scheme in hoping that 'all conflict of jurisdiction' had been avoided.[6]

It might have been expected that the precise delineation of federal and provincial powers and the absence of a formal bill of rights would have spared Canada the storms and battles that centred around the US Constitution from the Civil War until the Court Revolution of 1937. Instead we find a surprisingly parallel development. In place of the focus on the due-process clauses of the fifth and fourteenth amendments, the Canadian conflict revolved around the mode of judicial interpretation. Was the constitution to be regarded as an ordinary statute to be interpreted according to the ordinary rules of statutory construction? Or was it something more – a 'constitutional statute' – and therefore deserving of more beneficial interpretation than the normal rules of statutory construction might allow? The judicial approach to the interpretation of the Canadian constitution has fluctuated between these two extremes, and falls into three basic time periods, the second and third of which are central to an understanding of today's conflicts.

The first period stretches from 1867 to the mid-1890s. The Privy Council tended to construe the legislative powers of the federal Parliament broadly. In particular it conceded in full the federal government's general power to legislate for the 'Peace, Order, and good Government of Canada.'[7]

The second period began about 1896 and lasted till the Great Depression. There was during this period a notable contraction of federal legislative powers and a concomitant assertion of provincial rights. The Privy Council, under Lord Watson, and Lord Haldane, his spiritual successor, cut down the federal government's general legislative power in deference to the heads of provincial power enumerated in section 92. The federal government was not to legislate under the general power in section 91 where the effect was to 'trench' upon the provincial classes of subjects.[8] Lord Haldane, indeed, went further than Lord Watson and enunciated the so-called 'emergency' doctrine. The federal general legislative power under section 91 was strictly confined to use in periods of national emergency such as war, famine, or pestilence.[9]

Further, there was a federal power under section 132 to legislate to implement the obligations of Canada or any province 'as part of the British Empire ... arising under Treaties between the Empire and such Foreign Countries.' This was held not to cover obligations entered into by Canada herself in her new status as an international person, notwithstanding the Privy Council's express notice of the constitutional developments in Dominion status since the enactment of the BNA Act.[10]

Even the federal government's head of power over the 'regulation of trade and commerce,' a power which has proved so fertile a source of federal legislative authority in the United States, was deprived of any real significance. Lord Haldane ruled in the *Board of Commerce* Case that the trade and commerce power was available only to 'aid' the federal government in an exceptional situation to exercise the power conferred by the general language of section 91. Where no power was possessed by the federal Parliament independently of the trade and commerce section, the trade and commerce section could not operate. So low indeed did the trade and commerce power fall that Chief Justice Anglin of the Canadian Supreme Court was moved to protest that it had been denied all efficacy as an independent enumerative head of Dominion legislative jurisdiction.[11]

There were two key figures in this evolution: the intellectually dominant Anglo-Scottish judges, Lord Watson, and his disciple, Lord Haldane. Haldane had been a reformist minister in Asquith's Liberal government. He was a philosopher in his own right, and had studied philosophy in Edinburgh and in Göttingen. In the period between his two terms as Lord Chancellor, he published two major philosophical texts, *The Reign of Relativity* (1921) and *The Philosophy of Humanism* (1922). Haldane was associated more particularly with German philosophy, and the restatement of Hegelian ideas in the light of modern scientific work. He was, however, also known to be familiar with the liberal pluralist ideas of the Scottish philosopher, Figgis.

A judge is the product of his general education quite as much as of his more narrowly specialized professional legal training and experience. It would have been unlikely for Watson and Haldane to put aside altogether earlier liberal and pluralist predilections. Their general intellectual formation undoubtedly encouraged them to give effect to the more enlightened policies of latter-day British imperialism. These encouraged the ethnic and cultural particularism of non-British groups that had been absorbed into the empire by annexation or conquest. Liberal pluralism pointed to the judicial tolerance of self-government and self-legislation at the local level.

In Canada this meant a deliberate decentralization of the federal system in favour of the provinces. This tendency would be reinforced by fostering local (here, Quebec) self-determination as much as possible – as a means of compensating for the harshness of Quebec's original enforced absorption into British North America. In order to achieve such an interpretation of the BNA Act, Lord Watson and Lord Haldane and their colleagues on the Privy Council had to indulge in considerable judicial ingenuity. They executed considerable extensions beyond the actual text of the constitution – as English-Canadian academic critics from the 1930s onwards have claimed. In retrospect, given today's tensions between Ottawa and Quebec (and the provinces generally), this may all seem rather prophetic. In any case, they acted in the spirit of the fundamental compromises preceding the formal adoption of the constitutional text of 1867.

After the successive passing of Lord Watson and Lord Haldane from the benches of the Privy Council for Canadian constitutional cases, there was from the 1930s onwards a new trend in judicial interpretation. It bore a strong resemblance to the original, centralizing imperative of the first post-Confederation tribunals.

Thus Lord Sankey declared in the *Persons* Case in 1930: 'The [BNA] Act planted in Canada a living tree capable of growth and expansion within its natural limits. The object of the Act was to grant a Constitution to Canada ... Their Lordships do not conceive it to be the duty of this Board – it is certainly not their desire – to cut down the provisions of the Act by a narrow and technical construction, but rather to give it a large and liberal interpretation.'[12] Admittedly, Lord Sankey cut down the sweep of his comments by adding that he was not considering the respective legislative competences of the Dominion and of the provinces under sections 91 and 92 of the act. But in *British Coal Corporation* v. *The King*, he upheld the right of the Dominion Parliament to abolish appeals from Canadian courts to the Privy Council in criminal cases. He there quoted his own remarks in the *Persons* Case without the caveat as to sections 91 and 92, and expressly recognized that 'in interpreting a constituent or organic statute such as the [BNA] Act, that construction most beneficial to the widest possible amplitude of its powers must be adopted.'[13]

It was in the tradition of Lord Sankey that the Privy Council in 1947 approached the question of the legislative competence of the Dominion Parliament to abolish appeals from Canadian courts to the Privy Council in all classes of cases. The case did not directly concern sections 91 and 92 of the BNA Act, but principally section 101 of the act. The Privy Council approached most boldly the task of signing its own death warrant so far as Canadian appellate jurisdiction was concerned. 'It is ... irrelevant that the question is one that might have seemed unreal at the date of the [BNA] Act. To such an organic statute the flexible interpretation must be given which changing circumstances require.'[14]

The controversy over the special rôle of the Privy Council in the interpretation of the British North America Act was initiated by English-Canadian academic leaders in the 1930s and the 1940s. It necessarily centres around the period from 1896 onwards, and the judicial personalities of Lord Watson and Lord Haldane. As Dean (later Mr Justice) Vincent MacDonald contended, by treating the BNA Act as an ordinary statute without regard to the intentions of the 'fathers' of the constitution, the Privy Council after 1896 reached a 'result which the historian knows to be untrue,' and a constitution which '(rightly or wrongly) embodied a Centralized Federalism in which Dominion legislative power was of paramount importance ... has yielded a Decentralized Federalism in terms of legislative power; and one, moreover, that is ill-adapted to present needs.'[15]

Vincent MacDonald collected a long list of Dominion social and economic legislation held invalid as encroaching upon provincial powers under sections 92(13) and 92(16) or otherwise beyond the powers of the Dominion Parliament. It may be argued, however, that these are often not so much concrete jurisdictional conflicts as instances of private interest groups invoking constitutional law arguments to resist governmental regulation of whatever nature. In this case, they resisted federal regulation, with the element of Dominion-provincial differences tending to be artificial. It does not require a formal bill of rights or a due process clause in order for natural-law concepts of the proper limits of governmental activity *vis-à-vis* the private citizen or corporation to operate in constitutional law.

Granted the premise that the BNA Act is to be treated as an ordinary statute and not as a 'constitutional' statute, do the Privy Council decisions flow inevitably from the words of the BNA Act? Dean Kennedy was convinced that any hope that effect would be given to the intentions of the framers of the act was doomed to disappointment. The study of those intentions might be interesting, but was of no value except in showing the futility of the hope that the intentions and statute will accord. The Privy Council's approach was in accord with the 'rules of the legal game,'[16] according to Dean Kennedy:

After a careful examination of every case, in every jurisdiction, dealing with the interpretation of the Act, I venture to submit that in not one of them has the *ratio decidendi* depended on reasons external to the Act ... So generally uniform has been the approach of the judicial committee that, on the basis of it, I anticipated almost all these judgments except that on unemployment insurance, before their subject-matters were referred to the Supreme Court, and thence to London.[17]

But other commentators are not so certain as to the inevitability of the course of the Privy Council's decisions. Indeed, Professor Bora Laskin did not merely repudiate any idea of inevitability, but asserted, 'if anything, [the course of decisions] indicates conscious and deliberate choice of a policy which required, for its advancement, manipulations which can only with difficulty be represented as ordinary judicial techniques.'[18]

The ultimate appraisal of the Privy Council's contribution to the Canadian constitution as law-in-action must turn in considerable measure on two matters. One's attitude towards judicial legislation – judicial choice between conflicting policy alternatives – is central, as is one's attitude to the particular judicial policy choices made in specific cases. Part of the problem in Canada has stemmed from the persistence of the traditionalist assertion that the judicial rôle is a purely mechanical one and that there is not, and has not been, any scope for judicial policy-making. It is not without significance that the controversy over the Privy Council's interpretation of the BNA Act should all too frequently take the form of a dispute over alternative rules of statutory construction rather than over the actual consequences to Canadian life flowing from the individual decisions.

The need for a critical examination of the values employed by judges in making their decisions has often been obscured by unproductive wrangling over the formulae in which the judges subsequently embody those values. However, individual members of the Privy Council have occasionally adverted directly to the consequences of their decisions. Thus Lord Haldane, in summing up in 1923 the work of his predecessor and mentor Lord Watson, paid eloquent tribute:

As a result of a long series of decisions, Lord Watson put clothing upon the bones of the Constitution, and so covered them over with living flesh that the Constitution of Canada took a new form. The Provinces were recognized as of equal authority coordinate with the Dominion, and a long series of decisions were given by him which solved many problems, and produced a new contentment in Canada with the Constitution they had got in 1867. It is difficult to say what the extent of the debt was that Canada owes to Lord Watson.[19]

Seen against a background of developing Canadian nationhood, the Privy Council's pendulum-like swings in judicial interpretation acquire a certain logical sequence.

The period from 1867 to 1896, represented by the Privy Council decision in *Russell* v. *The Queen*,[20] favoured a broad interpretation of Dominion powers even at the expense of the provinces. This coincides with the dominance of John A. Macdonald and the Conservative party. It was the era of the 'moving frontiers,' when the settlers advanced westward and northward, when the railway was pushed across the continent, and when new provinces were progressively admitted into Confederation as the settlers' frontiers extended. A strong centralized administration could aid and foster this expansion.

In the period from 1896 onwards, however, Lord Watson and then Lord Haldane and his successors restricted Dominion powers in favour of provincial rights. This was the period of Laurier and King, when the Liberal party depended on the French for its parliamentary majority far more than the Conservative party had ever done. It was a period introduced, appropriately enough, by the Manitoba education crisis. Laurier (a French Catholic himself) sacrificed short-range French Catholic interests in separate schools in Manitoba for the long-range safeguard for Quebec of the autonomy of provincial administrations against interference by Ottawa. This was what Dean Kennedy hailed as an 'experiment in sovereignty ... a serious contribution to the destruction of the Austinian idea. Every province is from one point of view at least – in relation to the federal government – an example of a group with a life and purpose of its own.'[21]

Thus, the provincial rights plea may frequently spring from deeply rooted claims for the treatment of problems at the local level. There are in Canada two distinct groups differing radically in language, religion, and social customs. Two distinct 'living laws' require a pluralist organization of national life with a large degree of policy-making located at the periphery rather than at the centre.[22]

The interdiction of the federal government's social and economic planning laws has not necessarily made a legislative no-man's land in these matters. For example, although the field of labour law seems effectively barred to the federal government,[23] most of the provinces have in fact legislated in this field.[24] There is also considerable scope for legislative co-operation between the federal government and the provinces, though the difficulties here should not be underestimated. The special position of French-Canadians and the Catholic church was recognized in 1774 with the passage of the Quebec Act. The denominational schools in the provinces were given special protection under section 93 of the BNA Act. Even the invalidation by the Privy Council of the Canadian 'New Deal' legislation introduced by the Conservative government of R.B. Bennett (which decision seemed to arouse more ire among the critics than any other) was largely an academic question by the time the decisions were given. The Conservative government had been defeated at the general elections, and Mackenzie King's government had referred its predecessor's legislation to the courts for an opinion.

The beginnings of a new favouring of Dominion legislative powers, evidenced in Lord Sankey's 'living tree' doctrine and the cases which followed it, presaged a new acceptance of the need for centralization of governmental decision-making power during the Great Depression.

The question arose in 1949 of what the Canadian Supreme Court would do as final appellate tribunal in its own right. For the period prior to the abolition of the appeal to London in 1949, the decisions of the Privy Council on the BNA Act did not differ substantially from decisions of the Canadian Supreme Court in the first instance. Dean Kennedy was at some pains to absolve the Canadian Supreme Court judges from any share of responsibility for the Privy Council's decisions: 'The Supreme Court is bound by the judgments of the Privy Council, and it must profess to follow them to the best of its ability. The generality of judicial methods observed by the judicial committee almost made the decisions of the supreme court inevitable.'[25]

This view was, however, strongly challenged by Professor Laskin. Although Chief Justice Anglin indicated opposition to the Watson-Haldane viewpoint, the views of Chief Justice Sir Lyman Duff were

not solely the result of the compulsion of Privy Council decisions. The 'locus classicus' accolade bestowed by the Privy Council [in 1937] on [Duff's] judgment in the *Natural Products Marketing Act*[26] reference may, in part, have been merely a self-serving tribute to a skillful and faithful exposition of its own course of decision but Sir Lyman showed, as early as the *Board of Commerce* case [in 1920][27], that he had embarked on that course as much by his own choice as by the dictate of *stare decisis*.[28]

The 'Canadianization' of the final apellate judicial system, finally achieved in 1949, was essentially a product of English-Canadian juridical nationalism. From the Quiet Revolution onwards, when the first detailed Quebec-based criticisms of Canadian federal institutions begin to appear, Quebec students often tended to look nostalgically to the era of the Privy Council's interpretation. They saw qualities of neutrality or intellectual detachment – and beyond that, of political magnanimity – thought to be displayed by that distant tribunal. In contrast, the Supreme Court of Canada – as a body wholly nominated and appointed by the federal executive – tended to be viewed in Quebec as being committed in advance to the same centralizing imperatives and determinedly non-pluralist constitutional philosophy as the other central government organs established under the BNA Act.

Any such Quebec attitudes were perhaps reinforced by the 1950s' decisions of the Supreme Court. English-Canadian lawyers characterized these with pride as civil-liberties decisions. French-Canadian lawyers viewed them as public-order decisions, or, at least, cases involving conflicts between interests in speech and communication and interests in community order. These decisions tended to be rendered, in cases arising from Quebec, by English-Canadian judicial majorities over the dissent of their French-Canadian colleagues. The decisions were often without benefit of sustained argument from Quebec civil-law jurisprudence[29] in the majority opinions. Such argument would seem basic not merely to the decision but also to the educational aspect of judicial decision-making. There is an obligation within a federal judicial system to explain and rationalize a decision to the constituent unit concerned. Mr Justice Felix Frankfurter of the US Supreme Court, a great civil libertarian himself, would no doubt have reached the same end-result. As a dedicated federalist, however, he would undoubtedly have produced for that result an intellectually persuasive and educational justification in liberal and pluralist terms.

The *Off-Shore Mineral Rights* Advisory Opinion Reference of 1967[30] may have been an error of political judgment on the part of the federal government (see chapter 4). The federal government decision to take the matter up with the Supreme Court took place at a very early stage in federal-provincial negotiation of the ownership and disposition of the key economic resources involved. The federal decision to go to court hardened negotiating positions in advance, and may thereby have prevented or delayed compromise solutions between the two levels of government. The Supreme Court's ruling, when it was eventually announced, simply confirmed Quebec and other provinces' reservations about the court. The Supreme Court did not attempt to educate or explain: The ruling seemed unsatisfactory in its reasoning and unabashedly centralist in its upholding of Ottawa's claims. We will see a number of similar decisions, and it is in this context that the provinces' disillusionment with the Supreme Court must be seen.

3
Quebec Constitutional Theory

The constitutional ideas of the Quiet Revolution era are the products, first of all, of the university community. This is perhaps not surprising if we remember that it took the Quiet Revolution itself to achieve for Quebec a permanent, career civil service with its own professional, higher administrative cadre. Nor should the emphasis upon constitutional solutions be surprising, in view of the classical education in Quebec institutions of higher learning and the dominant rôle of the law faculties and their graduates in Quebec political and social thinking.

The most articulate and comprehensive of the constitutional theorists of the early Quiet Revolution was Jacques-Yvan Morin. He was a young professor of public law at the *Université de Montréal* and later a *Parti québécois* member of the *Assemblée nationale*. He became house leader of the opposition while the party leader, René Lévesque, remained unsuccessful in his bid to win a seat. He became the deputy premier and Minister of Education in the Lévesque government. In the mid-1960s, when first formulating his theories, Professor Morin was still a federalist. His detailed proposals were advanced as modifications of the existing federal structures *within* Confederation. Morin, in fact, was the most sophisticated exponent at that time of a 'special constitutional status' for Quebec within Confederation.

Morin sought to put the Quiet Revolution in a historical perspective. He traced a century of tensions between English and French Canada. He saw an English-Canadian 'melting pot' conception of the assimilation of non-English immigrant groups into one Canadian 'nation.' Opposed to this he saw a rival French-Canadian conception involving, in Henri Bourassa's words of 1904, 'a Canadian nationalism founded on the duality of races and on the particular traditions that duality involves.'[1]

But as the principal cause of the conflicts of contemporary Canadian federalism Morin identified the Rowell-Sirois Commission Report, published in 1941. The report was in accord with English-Canadian ideology, and was influenced by 'New Deal' interventionist policies stemming ultimately from Keynesian economic theories. It became an official apologia for administrative efficacy and for the consequent centralization of governmental decision-making power – above all, economic and fiscal powers – to the federal government in Ottawa.[2] The commission in effect invited the provinces to renounce their sources of independent revenue and to remit all direct taxes to the federal government in return for subventions which would permit them to 'dispense the services required by the national norm.' Implicitly, as Morin saw it, the commission 'effaced all the constitutional evolution which, since 1883, had been favourable to decentralisation' in Canadian federalism. In this way, displacing the founding fathers of 1867 and Lords Watson and Haldane, Lord Keynes became the true father of Confederation.

Morin found the constitutional antipode to the Rowell-Sirois Commission in the Tremblay Commission which was established by the Duplessis government in 1953 and reported back to the Quebec government in 1956. The Tremblay Commission conceived of federalism as above all a solution to the problem of the co-existence within Canada of two collectivities of different origin and culture, each seeking to conserve its own identity.[3] In this perspective, one should not seek only to construct a technically efficacious state; one should also distribute the state functions and competences in such a way as to assure the parallel development of two collectivities. Quebec as the home of the French-Canadian nation was thus invested with a particular mission and could not give up its autonomy, for every federal intervention in domains touching culture risked imposing fashions of thinking and acting foreign to French Canada. The Tremblay Commission's conception of federalism was thus diametrically opposed to that of the Rowell-Sirois Commission. This was evident in its suggestion for the readaptation of the taxation system so that the provinces, with their responsibility in cultural and social matters, would maintain direct taxes and royalties from natural resources. The federal government (with its general economic responsibilities) would limit itself to collecting taxes bearing on the circulation of goods.

The Tremblay Commission's detailed recommendations in the taxation field were later to be embraced by Jean Lesage at the federal-provincial conferences of November 1963 and April 1964. He suggested that, as the first step in the new Pearson government's announced 'cooperative federalism,' the federal government should return to the provinces the direct taxes that Ottawa had appropriated to pay for the Second World War, and that Quebec should collect its own taxes.[4]

In political and institutional terms, Professor Morin spoke of the necessity for 'a new constitutional equilibrium' in place of the equilibrium of 1867 which he saw as definitely shattered. He spoke, first of all, of the notion of 'Associated States.' The two Canadian nations would each be represented by its own national state and associated for certain ends by the adoption of a constitutional pact, involving confederal institutions. Among these would be a unicameral legislature with elected representatives from the two associated states, and even if the representation therein were not equal, no law should enter into force unless approved by a double majority. The inspiration here seems to be the Austro-Hungarian *Ausgleich* of 1867, with the twin Austrian and Hungarian delegations.

The proposal, however, seemed at that stage – the mid-1960s – to be designed more as a talking or debating point, with the main proposal in fact being 'particular' constitutional status for Quebec, expressed as 'a form of dualism reconcilable with the federal *régime*.'[5] While Morin saw such particular status as an exception to the principle of equality of the member-states of a federation, he demonstrated, historically, that such a notion of constitutional particularity was common enough in continental European experience and had, indeed, roots that went back to the Roman Republic and the early Roman Empire. Particular status was also, as Morin pointed out, part of British Imperial and British Commonwealth constitutionalism. That was not necessarily surprising seeing that the British élites were so often formed by classical education, with exposure to Roman legal and constitutional history.[6] In fact, the whole history of the constitutional arrangement for Quebec as part of the British Empire was one of a particularized status in religious and civil law matters expressly guaranteed in the Capitulations of 1759 and 1760, the Treaty of Paris of 1763, and the Quebec Act of 1774.

Specifically, for Professor Morin, particular status for Quebec within Confederation involved a new division of legislative competences between Ottawa and Quebec. This would have given Quebec all powers necessary for regional planning and the development of natural resources, and for social security. There would be a new international rôle for Quebec involving the power to conclude treaties in domains flowing from provincial competences, and also the power to nominate half of the representatives of Canada to international organizations.

The key institutional proposals for a particular status, however, involved changes to the existing Senate and Supreme Court. All federal institutions were to reflect the bi-national character of the country. Hence the Senate, with competence over cultural questions and the protection of minority rights and the approval of nominations of diplomats and federal judges, was to represent directly the constituent units (provinces), preferably on the basis of equality between anglophone and francophone communities. The Supreme Court was to give way to a constitutional tribunal composed of an equal number of jurists from the anglophone and francophone communities, with these judges to be nominated by the provinces and elected by the Senate.[7] Proposals for such a tribunal as the arbiter of federal-provincial conflicts go back as early as Jean Lesage's suggestions to the federal-provincial conference of 1960. They are a recurrent and dominant theme thereafter in Quebec demands for change within Confederation; and it is not surprising that they should turn up as part of the 'particular constitutional status' package of the mid-1960s.

Another major figure in the formulation of the constitutional program of the Quiet Revolution was Claude Morin. Morin was a political theorist whose approach to federalism was developed – not through published works as with Professor Jacques-Yvan Morin – but in confidential civil-service memoranda and in prosaic and deliberately non-polemical inter-governmental conference briefs. Morin became, with the election of the Lesage government in 1960, the key provincial bureaucrat dealing with inter-governmental affairs and with Quebec-Ottawa relations in particular. He continued to serve in this rôle after the defeat of the Lesage government, retaining the same position of trust with the successor *Union nationale* governments, and with the Bourassa government elected in 1970.

Morin was apparently disillusioned with the results of attempts to negotiate special agreements or arrangements with Ottawa. There had been a pragmatic approach to the abstract concept of special status. The failure of this approach led him to quit the Quebec civil service and join the *Parti québécois* to run as a candidate in the provincial election. He eventually became Minister of Inter-Governmental Affairs in the Lévesque government. Morin had also been one of the architects of the Quebec-Ontario *entente cordiale* from the mid-1960s onwards. Perhaps his move from the civil service to the direct political action of public life also indicated unhappiness at Quebec's failure to rally significant support from the other provinces.

Morin's works were issued after he had put aside the cloak of civil service confidentiality. They reflected the increasing alienation of an evidently strong French-Canadian nationalist stemming from the failure of direct negotiation with Ottawa in constitutional matters. Quebec and France, as early as February 1965, had entered into bilateral accords for programs of exchanges and cooperation in educational and cultural matters. Morin saw Ottawa as pursuing a deliberate policy, through its *accord-cadre* with France of November 1965, of trying to control Quebec. Shutting it up in a general accord minimized Quebec gestures. Ottawa cited potential actions of the other provinces, and claimed they were animated by the same international preoccupations as Quebec. All this Morin saw as intended by Ottawa to demonstrate that Quebec couldn't pretend to any particularism whatsoever and was only a 'Province like the others.'[8]

The Confederation of Tomorrow Conference called by Premier Robarts of Ontario in November 1967 was seen by Morin as a response to the 'multiform persistence of a Quebec *malaise* and its verbal expression.' However, it was posited upon the ideas of peaceful coexistence of French-Canadians and English-Canadians, of bilingualism, and of regional inequalities, rather than upon any thought of constitutional revision as such. Nevertheless, in Morin's view, the Ontario initiative, which was 'not pleasing' to the federal government, finally induced Ottawa, 'in spite of initial hostility,' to undertake constitutional revision. This led to the first constitutional conference convoked by Prime Minister Pearson, in February 1968, and eventually to the Victoria Charter of 1971.

The Victoria Charter constitutional package Morin dismissed as a political *tour de force*: 'the Constitution could certainly be repatriated, revised, modernised – but the prior fundamental equilibrium of the country, or more exactly the disequilibrium which had led Quebec to put in cause the existing division of powers, couldn't be modified.'[9]

The Victoria Charter had 'aborted spectacularly' in June 1971 when the Bourassa government said 'No!' to the federal government's proposals 'whose family links with the Fulton-Favreau formula were so manifest.'[10] Quebec's continuing constitutional objective, from Lesage onwards, through Johnson and Bertrand to Bourassa, was a reform in depth of the Canadian political regime, not mere adjustments. Real reform would necessarily challenge the actual division of governmental competences between Ottawa and Quebec (and the other provinces).

Quebec's continuing constitutional attitude, according to Morin, displeased the federal government. Ottawa could not accept the existence of a serious problem in Quebec without putting in doubt the premises of its own program – the increase of bilingualism in Canada and the struggle against regional inequalities – which Ottawa hoped would satisfy French-Canadian ills. Morin saw the federal government as directing itself only reluctantly towards constitutional reform, and therefore trying to orient it in a way useful to itself.

It was clear the constitution had to be modernized, if only in its phraseology. One would have, one day, to 'repatriate' the BNA Act and thus be in a position to amend it in Canada, so why not do that at once? Hence, in the eyes of Ottawa, there was a need to establish a plan which, without formally refusing discussion on division of legislative powers, nevertheless proposed other priorities more conformable to federal wishes. Since the federal government felt it necessary to elaborate a neo-federalist doctrine based on future contingencies, several successive federal white papers were produced to that end.

Instead of the division of powers questions so crucial to Quebec, the Ottawa package deal for the Victoria Conference of 1971 deliberately chose other subjects: repatriation of the constitution; a formula for constitutional amendment; fundamental rights; linguistic rights; the preamble to the constitution; regional disparities; the mechanisms of federal-provincial relations, the Senate, and the judicial power. The only small concession by the federal government on the division of powers was the inclusion of international relations in the agenda. Even here, according to Morin, Ottawa was only discussing the matter because of its difficulties with Quebec on the subject. When the Quebec government officially rejected the Victoria Charter on 23 June 1971, its communiqué declared: 'This decision [the refusal] stems from the necessity to establish clear and precise constitutional texts, thus avoiding transferring to the judicial power a responsibility which belongs, above all, to the political power, that is, to the elected representatives.'[11]

As Morin concluded, the Quebec government had finally understood that the Victoria Charter was unacceptable, since it did not resolve the problems which had earlier incited Quebec to request a revision of the Canadian political system. Quebec also took note that the federal government assumed that once the Victoria Charter was adopted, constitutional negotiation would be terminated for a long time. For English Canada, the Victoria Charter was in fact the new constitution.

Claude Morin's complaint was all the more significant because, though clearly a nationalist, he was also clearly a federalist working for constitutional adjustments to Quebec's special situation within the Canadian federal system. Throughout his career as a Quebec civil servant, the development of his political thinking has been recorded through a catalogue of specific issues of Quebec-Ottawa relations of the 1960s: off-shore mineral rights; the Ottawa-Hull region; the establishment and operation of a federal ministry of cultural affairs, communications, and manpower.

Traditional Quebec constitutional theory also developed during the Quiet Revolution. What was striking, in the debate over French Canada's rôle in Canadian federalism, was the conjunction of constitutional thinking derived from or influenced by the Quiet Revolution and more traditional Quebec constitutional thinking. Louis-Philippe Pigeon, the distinguished practitioner and professor (later Justice of the Supreme Court of Canada), advanced a plea in 1951 for eschewing any 'narrow and technical construction of the BNA Act' in favour of 'a much higher view ... recognis[ing] the implicit fluidity of any constitution.' The latter approach was conducive to 'the fundamental principle of provincial autonomy ... the essential condition of the Canadian confederation.'[12] Such thinking was amply reflected in the Tremblay Commission Report.

Marcel Faribault, a distinguished conservative constitutionalist, was head of the Quebec Conservatives in the 1968 federal election. In complete consistency with the philosophical attitudes of a lifetime of public service in Quebec, he called for substantial revisions of the division of legislative powers. In particular, he asked for marked accretions to the section 92 (provincial) powers at the expense of the federal government – all this in addition to a substantial restructuring of existing federal institutions like the Senate and the Supreme Court and the creation of a special Constitutional Court.[13]

Premier Daniel Johnson, at the federal-provincial conference in Ottawa in February 1968, called for a 'new constitution' for Canada. He was able to draw from both traditional Quebec thinking and the new constitutional ideas. He spoke of the 'impotence' of the then existing federal system, and found the root of the problem in its failure to reflect the cultural duality of Canada. A new constitution must provide for 'an authentic bilingualism and for a decentralized federal system in which intergovernmental cooperation replaces centralisation of powers.' He defined 'self-determination' as 'the power of decision of each group and its freedom to act, not only in its cultural life but in all aspects of its collective life,' and which he saw as leading on to the issue of the 'control ... over its government or governments.' In specifically rejecting any distinction between constitutional and cultural problems, he proceeded to identify the range of different constitutional options for Quebec: 'the constitutional framework in which the two societies can live or aspire to live: a unitary or a federal system; special status for the province in which the minority group is concentrated; or again, for the same part of the country, the status of an associate state; or finally, the status of an independent state.'[14]

Without specifically choosing between these options, Johnson argued for a new distribution of legislative powers, and specifically that the provinces should 'retain all powers not expressly granted to the central government.' He was expressly critical, in this regard, of the Supreme Court's interpretation of the existing divisions of competence, citing the then recent Supreme

Court ruling on off-shore mineral rights. Johnson also insisted that Quebec must 'regain full control over social security'; that Quebec must have, 'within the limits of Canadian foreign policy, a recognised capacity to negotiate and sign her own agreements with foreign governments on matters subject to her internal jurisdiction'; and that Quebec must have a constitutional rôle in regard to 'media for the dissemination of education and culture, particularly radio and television,' once again rejecting judicial rulings to the contrary.

Johnson's expressed reservations concerning federal proposals for a declaration of human rights in the constitutional charter itself stemmed in part from concern for the constitutional division of powers between the federal government and the provinces. And on the question of the federal government's tactics as to the timing and staging of the approach to constitutional change and the fixing of the priority issues he commented that 'a bill of rights should be the last part to be added to the constitution.'

Beyond that, 'because of the way in which the Supreme Court is constituted, it is difficult to accept this court as a constitutional tribunal of last resort. This important point will have to be included in a new constitution before we can concur in a constitutional bill of rights.'[15]

Let us now examine the 'second wave' of Quebec constitutional theory in the years after the Quiet Revolution. The intellectual and political reaction outside Quebec both to the first wave of Quiet Revolution constitutional thinking, and to the 'traditionalist' constitutional proposals was distressingly minor among English-speaking groups before the 1976 Quebec election. However, a constitutional debate of considerable intellectual proportions was initiated within Quebec itself, among key francophone groups.

Within the Bourassa government, the movement for an *aggiornamento* of Quebec society, directly inspired by the Quiet Revolution, brought an interest in over-all constitutional change outside the more restricted federal-provincial disagreements. Such change was seen as a solvent for more general community problems involving relations among private citizens, private groups, and the government. A cabinet sub-committee headed by Guy Saint-Pierre, the Minister for Commerce and Industry, was asked to examine existing Quebec governmental institutions and recommend reforms and modernization in the light of the experience of Quebec, the other provinces, the federal government, and other countries, notably the United States, France, and West Germany.

M Saint-Pierre had keen practical sense, and an academic and professional background in engineering and military science. His report, *La réforme des institutions politiques québécoises*, filed in June 1975, amply reflected the blend of the theoretical and the empirical. One part of the project was concerned with what might be called the purely honorific trappings of government, such as the 'head of state' within Quebec. The report considered the notion of replacing the office of Lieutenant-Governor with a president of a Quebec republic still operating within the Canadian federal system. The idea had an element of flexibility that recalled those imaginative improvisations of the old British Colonial Office.

The Saint-Pierre group also considered the transformation of the Quebec executive from a parliamentary to a presidential-style system (whether American, French, or German). The group also examined the reform of the *Assemblée nationale* itself in order to lighten the parliamentary rôle of ministers (including provision for extra-parliamentary ministers) and increase the rôle of back-benchers and parliamentary commissions.[16] The Bourassa government's preoccupation with 'language' issues flowing from Bill 22, and its 1976 defeat, meant, unfortunately, that the group's detailed recommendations were never officially released and, of course, never acted upon by the Quebec government.

Other 'second-wave' constitutional ideas stem mainly from non-official, academic sources. The Lévesque government is officially committed to constitutional separatism. It is hardly concerned with constitutional changes and reforms within the existing federal system, but only (in public at least) with the modalities of a Quebec departure from Canadian Confederation. Some Quebec opposition groups within the *Assemblée nationale*, however, began to pick up the cause of constitutional amendment within Confederation.

Professor Jacques Brossard of the Law Faculty of the *Université de Montréal* was certainly the most prolific of the second-wave writers, and he has had a special interest in comparative law and comparative federalism. Many publicists, whether francophone or anglophone, have ventured into eclectic jurisprudence in recent years to justify their own special solutions for the ills of Canadian federalism today. Professor Brossard, however, was neither a latter-day convert to comparative law, nor an 'instant' expert with sweeping generalizations on comparative federal experience on the basis of slender knowledge.

As early as 1967 Professor Brossard was looking to the practice of other countries for a critique of the current Ottawa policies in relation to the exercise of the federal foreign affairs power when it touched provincial legislative competence under section 92.[17] Professor Brossard was also one of the earliest and most thorough of the Quebec critics of the constitutional performance of the Supreme Court of Canada. He based his 1968 recommendations for change in the court statute, including the creation of a special constitutional court, directly on foreign – and especially continental European – experience.[18]

But Professor Brossard is not an international lawyer, and his 1976 study on the accession to sovereignty on the part of Quebec[19] perhaps worried too much about such an artificial distinction as that between 'nation' and 'people' which could hardly be solved by application of strictly *a priori* reasoning.

Nationalism, liberalism, and independence were a triad of historical forces unloosed by the French Revolution and the Napoleonic wars. They dominated political and legal development in Western Europe throughout the nineteenth century and to the outbreak of the First World War. But the pathological excesses of extreme nationalism between the two world wars caused the idea to fall into a certain public disrespect and disfavour after the Second World War. This induced the drafters of the United Nations Charter and similar international documents of the immediate post-war era to eschew the use of the term 'nation' wherever possible, in favour of euphemisms like 'people.'

Thus both the United Nations Charter and the UN General Assembly's Declaration on Friendly Relations and Cooperation among States (1970) spoke of 'self-determination of peoples,' instead of the older notion of national self-determination. They never defined precisely what a 'people' was, nor the criteria for identifying a 'people' as such. Nor do they indicate how 'self-determination' should finally manifest itself. As a strictly *a priori* concept, 'people' was just as vague and imprecise as 'nation' was before it. It seemed to be viewed by its UN drafters as more or less synonymous or interchangeable with 'nation,' but without the possible pejorative associations of the term 'nation.'

But there is no particular practical difficulty in defining either 'people' or 'self-determination of peoples.' The latter are those historical instances of the process of decolonization and independence after the Second World War in Asia, Africa, Latin America, and the Caribbean. The usage was thus limited to cases of 'salt-water' colonialism where a European country was separated by an ocean from its colonial territory. This definition of 'self-determination of peoples' had nothing at all to say concerning its potential application to non-colonial situations, whether to inter-group relations within a wholly European or European-settled state, or to a post-colonial succession state, or to the relations between several such succession states.

Professor Brossard's study was not any more helpful than the official United Nations definitions or actual United Nations practice in understanding the general legal relevance or the actual legal implications of the international law principle of 'self-determination of peoples' for the relations of Quebec or French Canada generally to federal Canada as a whole. Presumably so far as the customary-law principle remains in force, French Canada is entitled to invoke the principle of national self-determination *vis-à-vis* English-speaking Canada. But there is absolutely nothing in that principle requiring its application to effect the fission or break-up of an existing plural state. Presumably federalism and the newer experiments in institutionalizing pluralism within a single state or political unit would be legally perfectly compatible with its imperative.

Professor Brossard was most helpful in his discussion of the procedures for any Quebec accession to full sovereignty and independence *vis-à-vis* Canada.[20] This would be achieved only upon an express mandate secured in popular referendum. There is nothing to require or to suggest that it be achieved hurriedly or in one single legislative act. Professor Brossard discussed various historical examples of secession, separatism, and fission of states (terms without a precise legal connotation). He seemed to recommend a gradual approach following full diplomatic discussion and negotiation with Canada as a whole.

Professor Gérard Bergeron of the *Université Laval* in Quebec City, and sometime guest editorial writer for *Le Devoir* of Montreal, offered some concrete formulation of the concept of 'souveraineté-association' being sponsored by the Lévesque government. Professor Bergeron's project for a 'Canadian Commonwealth' would involve the juridical association of a state of Canada (federal and thus decentralized) and a state of Quebec (unitary and centralized). The official language of Canada would be English and of Quebec French, with both languages official at the Commonwealth level. Only the Commonwealth would have full sovereignty in the sense of international law.

Professor Bergeron's models seemed to be from continental Europe, especially the Austro-Hungarian Empire from 1867 to 1918. His proposal involved, at the Commonwealth level, a directorial *Council* selected from the central legislature (*Diet*) and functioning as a sort of continuing central executive. The central Diet would be selected on a regional and population basis, with Quebec deputies forming at least thirty per cent of the membership. Professor Bergeron did not limit his constitutional commentaries to his 'Canadian Commonwealth' project. In the spirit of the DeBané-Asselin dissent to the Molgat-MacGuigan Report he advocated recognition of a fundamental right of self-determination for the Quebec people in the existing federal system; and he was very critical of the existing Senate ('not a Chamber of federated states') and Supreme Court ('the strict creature of the central government, deprived of the prestige of the Supreme Court in Washington').[21]

Dean Gérald Beaudoin of the law faculty of the *Université d'Ottawa*, was named in August 1977 as one of the two Quebec members of the federal Commission on National Unity (Pépin-Robarts Commission). While he seemed to put aside as politically unsaleable the notion of a 'special' or 'particular' constitutional status for Quebec within Canadian confederation, he advanced certain proposals for a fuller involvement of the provinces in existing federal institutions.[22] Judges of the Supreme Court of Canada should continue to be named by the federal government, but those federal nominations should also require ratification either by a Senate reformed in such a way as more fully to represent the provinces or else by some other process involving participation of the provincial authorities. He also felt that federal nominations of ambassadors and of heads of crown corporations should be submitted to ratification by a reformed Senate, and that provincial Lieutenant-Governors or Heads-of-State should be named by the provinces. In addition, he was critical of the language and styling of the present federal constitutional charter ('inelegant and impregnated with colonialism') and of its failure to 'refer expressly to the two Founding Nations.'

Professor André Tremblay of the Faculty of Law of the *Université de Montreal* rejected both Quebec secession and an economic or other form of 'association' between Quebec and federal Canada. He felt that both these ideas were incapable of being imposed by Quebec on English Canada. Professor Tremblay tried instead to spell out the details of a new 'third option' within Canadian Confederation, involving the re-ordering of existing federal institutions which he charges as being 'perceived by Francophones as representing Anglophonic Canada.'[23] Such reforms must 'guarantee the equality of the status of Quebec.'

Professor Tremblay believed that, even a decade earlier, Quebec could have been satisfied with a 'particular' constitutional status giving Quebec exclusive jurisdiction over communications, immigration, and family questions. By 1978 a new 'decentralized federalism' would have to involve express constitutional recognition of the existence of the two cultural groups which have founded Canada, and of the equality of the two groups. (He rejected any notion of the constitutional equality of the existing ten provinces, or even of the somewhat larger 'regions' within the new, five-region

Canada proposed by some English-speaking provincial leaders.) Professor Tremblay would concede full liberty to each of the two cultural groups to endow itself with its own distinctive political institutions (for example, a presidential system for Quebec).

He would make of the federal government of Canada a government of named, delegated powers only. He would also reform existing federal institutions so that, for example, a directly elected federal parliament would be constituted on a forty-sixty francophone-anglophone basis, and the Supreme Court of Canada would give way to a 'bicultural tribunal' charged with the interpretation of the constitution and the bill of rights. While Professor Tremblay's views were formulated in his academic and professional capacity, he became in the spring of 1978 head of a new policy advisory group to the new Quebec Liberal leader, Claude Ryan.

Claude Ryan was André Laurendeau's successor as director of the prestigious *Le Devoir* of Montreal in 1963 and held that post until his resignation to contest the Quebec Liberal leadership early in 1978. He was one of the most influential figures in Quebec public life of the 1960s when the Quiet Revolution was occurring. Mr Ryan maintained his intellectual authority in the 1970s in part through his signed editorial columns in *Le Devoir* which took clear positions on almost every major political and social and cultural issue of the day. But he was also consulted on a confidential basis by Quebec premiers, ministers, and opposition leaders on major policy decisions and on the range of policy options in advance of those decisions. As a result, it is often difficult to separate Ryan's personal philosophy and political preferences from official Quebec policy at any time.

It is known from his editorials that Mr Ryan opposed Quebec's acceptance of both the early Fulton-Favreau formula for constitutional amendment and the later Victoria Charter of 1971 which included provision for the 'patriation' of the BNA Act and a revised version of the Fulton-Favreau formula.[24] In fact, Ryan was in the vanguard of the reaction against both these federal initiatives by French-Canadian intellectuals who felt that they would put Quebec's special claims in a constitutional strait-jacket before they had been recognized or accepted by English-Canada.

On the adoption of the French language as the official language of Quebec, Ryan endorsed the general principle as recommended by the Gendron Commission Report presented on 31 December 1972 and incorporated as the key element in Bill 22. Ryan's support was conditional upon certain other elements: recognition at the same time of a privileged status for the English language in Quebec, and the institution of rational and objective criteria for the legislative and administrative application of the French language norm in Quebec.

He was, on the latter ground, critical of Bill 22. There was an uneasy political compromise in chapter V of that bill between maternal language and language competence as the condition for admission to English-language public schools in Quebec. This opened the way, in Ryan's view, to wide-spread evasions – that in fact occurred – of the spirit of the bill and its intention to make French the official language of Quebec. But he was also, on the former ground, critical of Bill 101 which seemed to him to restrict and confine unnecessarily the specially privileged status reserved for the English language in Quebec at the same time that French was proclaimed as the official language of the province. (Bills 22 and 101 are examined in chapter 6.)

Ryan had given a last-minute editorial endorsement to the *Parti québécois* immediately before the 1976 election; but this was based on the domestic policies and administration of the outgoing Bourassa government and was in no way an endorsement of the separatist policies of the *Parti québécois* which were, in any case, muted during the election campaign.[25] The election of the Lévesque government was followed by the introduction of plans for a referendum on Quebec separation from Canada or at least on a new form of 'souveraineté-association' on a basis still to be formulated. A break between Ryan and the government became inevitable in view of Ryan's commitment to the federal principle and his reaction to what he felt to be the unnecessary rigidity and harshness of Bill 101 toward the English-language minority in Quebec. Mr Ryan's resignation from *Le Devoir* was followed by his election as provincial Liberal leader three months later on 15 April 1978.

A collection of documents issued by Ryan on the eve of his election as party leader was entitled simply 'Reflections on the challenges of the next few years.'[26] He quite properly eschewed detailed proposals for constitutional change which would hardly be timely or prudent for someone not even yet a member of the Quebec legislature. Nevertheless, these documents gave some indication of Ryan's thinking in his impending transition from philosopher-critic and 'candid friend' of Quebec governments to political leader in his own right.

He avoided categorical demands for a wholesale re-writing of the BNA Act and for fundamental recasting of existing federal institutions. However, he did identify key areas of political tension within the Canadian federal system today. He noted the invocation by the federal government of its 'general' power under section 91 to intervene in recent years in domains of provincial competence, the existing division of fiscal resources between the federal government and the provinces, and the existing mechanism of constitutional arbitration between the provinces and Ottawa.

Ryan spoke of Quebec as 'the principal home of the French life in Canada,' and of the distinctiveness of Quebec in relation to the rest of Canada in terms 'not only of its language, but also of its spirit.' He signalled the need for 'firmer and more explicit guarantees' for Quebec and for the 'French fact' within Quebec, but recognized unequivocally the need for the 'maintenance of a federal Parliament endowed with real powers and of a united Canada.' Was that an implied rebuke on Ryan's part to some of the more vociferous English-speaking critics of our federal system today? And Ryan rejected explicitly 'the old *cliché* that the Quebecers were more or less forced to enter Confederation in 1867.'

On the vexed 'language' issue Ryan called for a 'more explicit recognition for Francophones of their language rights within the federal administration and in the other Provinces,' and acknowledges the 'ever more numerous Anglophones of the other Provinces who accept henceforward the French fact as one of the most precious attributes of this country.' Within Quebec, Ryan emphasized the sociological (extra-constitutional) special status of Quebec inside Canadian federalism. This was reflected in his insistence that the French language, as proclaimed in Bill 22 and Bill 101, must remain the official language of Quebec.

He accepted the incremental progression expressed in the movement from Bill 22 to Bill 101 and the fundamental sociological premise on which the two laws rest – the 'French fact' in Quebec. As editor of *Le Devoir* he had criticized details of Bill 22, and he had far stronger misgivings about certain sections of Bill 101. He criticized the 'useless linguistic gendarmerie' and the recourse to coercive measures for the implementation of the French language (rather than the persuasive methods recommended by the Gendron Commission Report in 1972); the 'abusive interdiction of English' under Bill 101; the delegation to a single minister in charge or to the Quebec language authority of powers which, in Ryan's view, should be exercised only by the Quebec cabinet as a whole; the restrictions on access to English-language schools in Quebec for anglophones from other provinces or from abroad; and the attempt, by legislative indirection in Bill 101, to repeal or amend section 133 of the BNA Act insofar as it applied to the Quebec legislature and to the Quebec courts and to the use of English therein. Ryan would also insert provisions in the BNA Act and in Bill 101 to guarantee the language rights of the English-language minority in Quebec.

But Ryan seemed to agree that a great social revolution was effected in Quebec under the two bills – in the guise of a linguistic reform. This revolution he saw as the second or delayed wave of the modernization inaugurated by Jean Lesage and the Quiet Revolution; and he noted the economic and social implications of both bills when he emphasized the need for representation – 'in a reasonable proportion' – of French-Canadians in managerial posts in companies with head offices in Quebec and even in companies head-quartered outside Quebec.

Acceptance by English-Canadians of the main philosophical principle of Quebec's special language legislation – the primacy of the French language in Quebec – though not necessarily of all its applications or administration, may be the key to Ryan's 'new moral and political *entente*' that would fully involve Quebec within a united Canada. There was therefore good political sense in the federal government's refusal to launch a guerrilla war of litigation before the federal courts against the constitutionality of either bill. Ottawa in effect left correction of alleged abuses in both these laws to the operation of the ordinary political processes within Quebec and to judicial review through litigation in Quebec – as witness the two landmark decisions rendered by Chief Judge Jules Deschênes of the *Cour supérieure* of Quebec on the two Quebec language laws[27] (see chapter 6).

4
Quebec and Provincial Powers

The Quiet Revolution brought in its wake an increasingly critical examination by Quebec of the nature and character of the Canadian constitutional system and of the extent to which it acted as a barrier to realization of French-Canadian demands for national self-determination.

It was a period of intellectual *risorgimento* in the French-Canadian universities and in the Quebec provincial civil service which had begun for the first time to gain a professional, specialist, technocratic character in the wave of reform following the passing of the *Union nationale* régime in 1960. In the universities and in legal doctrine the new period of intellectual enlightenment brought forth a philosophical debate centering around the new theoretical concepts of a 'special' or 'particular' constitutional status for Quebec within Canadian federalism. When the debate went beyond that but still stopped short of an outright break with the existing federal system, it sometimes advanced an 'associate state' status for Quebec.

The Quebec provincial civil service produced a highly pragmatic technocratic élite which quickly challenged its federal counterpart. The debate was brought down from a high level of generality and abstraction to specific issues in Ottawa-Quebec relations, as the new Quebec team attempted to match Ottawa with a detailed argument in each case.

The new Quebec approach was helped by the fact that the BNA Act, like all other functioning federal charters, allocates law-making competences between the two levels of government. It does so by the use of general and open-ended categories rendered precise and meaningful through application. Even the assumed sophistication of the BNA Act in comparison with other such charters – it has separate lists of federal and provincial powers and a few concurrent powers – could not overcome the necessity of remaining general in definitions of power so as to avoid an endless catalogue.

Nor of course could the drafters of the 1860s foresee every future situation and devise appropriate verbal solutions in advance. They could not anticipate that, after a century of application, their attempts.at *a priori* division of federal and provincial powers into watertight compartments would become dated. Wise community policy-making today requires cooperative decision-making between the different levels of government, and not abstract legal battle.

Recognition of this truth has come only slowly, by trial and error, during inter-governmental conflicts in the 1960s and early 1970s. There has been a dialectical development in the confrontations between the different levels of government during that era. Quebec-Ottawa conflicts have been at the core of this process, though it has by no means been limited to them.

The English-speaking provinces have also participated from time to time, or have rallied to the Quebec side or been joined by Quebec in disputes that they themselves initiated with Ottawa. The examples that follow illustrate this dialectical process in constitutional law. Although all drawn from the period of the Quiet Revolution and later, they differ only in degree of intensity and in the speed with which the political events have been consummated.

The making and implementation of treaties was a subject of controversy between Ottawa and Quebec in the 1960s. In 1937 the Privy Council handed down a decision concerning the treaty section of the BNA Act. The BNA Act contains only one section bearing on foreign affairs, namely the brief and ill-fated section 132: 'The Parliament and Government of Canada shall have all Powers necessary or proper for performing the Obligations of Canada or of any Province thereof, as Part of the British Empire, towards Foreign Countries arising under Treaties between the Empire and such Foreign Countries.'

Unfortunately section 132 expressly limits the federal power of implementing treaty obligations to the case of 'British Empire' treaties. When Canada became a Confederation in 1867 her foreign relations were administered by Great Britain, which entered into treaties on behalf of Canada as for all other parts of the empire. Section 132 thus describes completely the foreign affairs power of Canada in 1867. The Imperial government had the monopoly of treaty-making power in respect to Canada. Section 132 gives the Canadian federal legislature treaty-implementation power in respect to treaties so entered into by Britain on behalf of Canada.

The power of the British government to enter into treaties on behalf of Canada effectively disappeared by the early 1930s through evolving constitutional custom. The issue was then raised whether section 132 could not be interpreted so as to confer treaty-*implementation* power on the Canadian legislature in respect to treaties *made* by Canada in her own right in her new capacity as a full international person. The Imperial Privy Council, after some hesitation, finally said 'No!' The decision was given in a major opinion – the *Labour Conventions* opinion[1] – rendered in 1937, and remaining law ever since. Section 132 has thus become, for all practical purposes, a constitutional dead letter, since no 'British Empire' treaties have been made for Canada since the 1920s.

What has happened then to the Canadian foreign affairs power? In the *Labour Conventions* case, the Supreme Court of Canada, as court of first instance[2], had seemed to suggest that the treaty-*making* power for Canada remained with the federal government. The Privy Council, sitting as court of appeal from the Supreme Court of Canada in the *Labour Conventions* case, actually held however that the treaty-*implementation* power – the point directly at issue in the case – was constitutionally divided between the federal government and the provinces. The division depended on whether the subject matter of the treaty came under the federal or provincial heads of power in sections 91 and 92.

The Privy Council's judgment in the *Labour Conventions* case in 1937 was very well received in Quebec. It was viewed there as protecting provincial legislative powers and competence against unwarranted legislative encroachments by the federal government under the guise of exercise of the foreign affairs power. The judgment was, however, strongly criticized by a number of English-speaking scholars, in the spirit of the markedly centralizing philosophy then current in English-speaking universities in Canada.

Indeed, at one time in the early 1950s, after the final abolition of the appeal from Canada to the Privy Council, it looked as if the English-speaking majority on the Supreme Court might be moved to over-rule the *Labour Conventions* judgment, if given the opportunity to do so. However, this period now seems passed, for the *Labour Conventions* decision, in the present era of more pluralistic federalism in Canada, looks in retrospect perhaps wiser than when it was first pronounced in 1937.

The treaty-*implementation* power, following the *Labour Conventions* rationale, is now constitutionally divided between the federal government and the provinces, following the division of powers in sections 91 and 92; but the same is not necessarily true of the treaty-*making* power. In the full spirit of French-Canadian nationalism, some Quebec jurists cited various examples drawn from the practice of other federal states as diverse as Imperial Germany, Switzerland, and the Soviet Union. They began demanding a right of the province itself to make treaties in areas of subject matter falling within provincial powers as defined in section 92. A constitutional crisis arose – proceeding from the abstract legal argument to the concrete governmental claim – over education.

Quebec pointed out in the mid-1960s that the federal government, while always willing to conclude cultural agreements with English-speaking countries, had not attempted to conclude cultural agreements with French-speaking countries. Quebec claimed the constitutional authority, in her own right, to conclude cultural-exchange agreements with France and '*la Francophonie*' in general.[3]

In 1965 the African francophone country of Gabon invited the government of Quebec to send an official delegate to a conference of education ministers from the French-speaking countries. It did not, however, at the same time invite the federal government to transmit the Gabon invitation to the Quebec government. The federal government and Prime Minister Pearson were so annoyed that the federal government broke off diplomatic relations altogether with Gabon.

In retrospect, the reaction of the federal government in the affair of Gabon may seem to have been rather too hasty or exaggerated – escalating a minor incident into a major diplomatic confrontation. The conference in Gabon, after all, concerned only educational exchanges, and no concrete international-law consequences or obligations flowed from its proceedings. In addition, it was soon found that other provinces had concluded various trans-national agreements with various countries. These had covered educational exchanges and a whole host of other matters such as roads and highway construction, bridge-building, fire-fighting, reciprocal enforcement of maintenance orders, and the like. The number of such agreements effected by the individual provinces ran probably into the hundreds, and all these without any complaint or protest or attempt at political reprisal on the part of the federal government.

However, some of the Quebec leaders concerned had offended against accepted canons of federalism. They seemed to take a special delight in irritating the federal government in their actual manner of conducting negotiations with Gabon and other francophone countries. They had, for example, emphasized the flying of the Quebec provincial flag and the use of other essentially nineteenth-century trappings of sovereignty.

The federal government had itself also behaved very badly from time to time. An official invitation from Tunisia to Quebec, to take part in a cultural meeting, was formally delivered by the Tunisian government to the federal government for transmission to the Quebec government. This was in accordance with the protocol insisted upon by the federal government in the Gabon affair. The invitation was reportedly lost by the federal government until the meeting in Tunisia was over.

After these displays of inter-governmental friction, calmer counsel began to prevail. For future cultural exchanges the federal government, under the initiative of the External Affairs Secretary, Paul Martin, worked out an umbrella agreement with France. The agreement established the general principle of cultural exchange between France and Canada and expressly conceded to Quebec and France the right to make individual exchange agreements on a direct bilateral basis. This all fell within the overall framework of the umbrella agreement between Canada and France.[4]

As for the myriad provincial trans-national agreements already concluded in areas other than cultural exchanges, the pragmatic compromise that seemingly emerged was a simple *laissez-faire* principle. The principle applied where there was no specific international-law obligation imposed between the provinces and foreign countries or between the provinces and member-states of other federal systems. Such agreements did not concern Ottawa as long as they rested for their practical enforcement (as they invariably did) on their reasonableness and common sense and on the mutual, reciprocal interests of the signatories. The only question was whether the subject matter of the agreements fell within the heads of provincial power in section 92.

Quebec and other provinces resented Ottawa's attempts in 1967-68 to claim a monopoly of competence over off-shore mineral rights. The off-shore oil deposits issue arose as a dispute between the federal government and those provinces having a coastal shoreline. It concerned the respective constitutional competences and legislative jurisdiction in regard to the development and exploitation of mineral sources – and especially oil – under the territorial waters, contiguous zones, and continental shelf of Canada. The dispute was basically economic. It concerned the respective rights to grant licenses to private companies to exploit the mineral resources and oil deposits, and the rights to collect the licensing fees and royalties accruing from such development by private companies. Behind this was a federal-provincial economic conflict involving potentially hundreds of millions of dollars per year.

The federal government claimed a monopoly of constitutional competence over underwater oil and mineral deposits, and referred the matter to the Supreme Court for an advisory opinion. Ottawa relied upon a claimed general residual legislative power under Section 91 and somewhat vaguely, on the foreign affairs power under the constitution. Six provinces – British

Columbia, Ontario, and the four Atlantic provinces – formally contested in the Supreme Court the legality of the federal government's claims. Quebec, though not formally joining with the other six provinces, was known to take an even stronger constitutional position against the federal government.

The opinion rendered by the Supreme Court of Canada, *Reference re Ownership of Off-Shore Mineral Rights*, was odd in several respects. Though rendered by a seven-man bench of the Supreme Court, the judgment defied all previous Canadian Supreme Court and Commonwealth practice. It was anonymous and unsigned, being styled simply a 'Joint Opinion' without any formal identification of the authorship. There are reasons for suspecting on technical and stylistic grounds that the opinion was the work of two separate judges, one writing the first half and the other completing it.

Students of the work of the Supreme Court have been troubled, since the publication of the *Off-Shore Mineral Rights* opinion, as to the intellectual bases and the reasoning of certain of its parts. For example, in discussing the territorial sea the Supreme Court comments in its opinion: 'The rights in the territorial sea arise by international law and depend upon recognition by other sovereign states. Legislative jurisdiction in relation to the lands in question belongs to Canada which is a sovereign state recognized by international law and thus able to enter into arrangements with other states respecting the rights in the territorial sea.'[5]

Again, in relation to the continental shelf, the Supreme Court stated:

There are two reasons why British Columbia lacks the right to explore and exploit (the continental shelf) and lacks legislative jurisdiction:
1. The Continental shelf is outside the boundaries of British Columbia, and
2. Canada is the sovereign state which will be recognised by international law as having the rights stated in the Convention of 1958, and it is Canada, not the Province of British Columbia, that will have to answer the claims of other members of the international community for breach of the obligations and responsibilities imposed by the Convention.[6]

These statements suggest that the Supreme Court was making the fatal equation between jurisdiction in international law in relation to foreign countries and internal law jurisdiction between the federal and provincial governments. That there is no logical or necessary connection between the two is the core of the Privy Council's ruling in the 1937 *Labour Conventions* case. There is also the further policy-type argument that considerations of liberal pluralism within a federal state may well demand that the federal state submit to inconveniences from time to time in the practical conduct of foreign policy. This means observing provincial powers and not attempting inroads purporting to be based on the federal foreign affairs power. It strains credulity to believe that the Supreme Court intended in the *Off-Shore Mineral Rights* reference to overrule the *Labour Conventions* decision *sub silentio*. One's conclusion must therefore be that the reference to the *Labour Conventions* case was not properly presented, at least to a court whose opportunities of ruling on international law issues are few and far between. This apparent non sequitur in the *Mineral Rights* reference was therefore arrived at by the Court *per incuriam*. This is rather startling in view of the enormous economic and financial interests turning on the outcome of the court's opinion, and in view also of its implications for the future of Canadian federalism.

The criticism of the *Mineral Rights* opinion by the six provinces and Quebec clearly weakened the Supreme Court's prestige and authority. This was at a time when it was already under attack, on other grounds, for its allegedly centralizing philosophy and for its decisions in favour of the federal government. The publication of the *Off-Shore Mineral Rights* opinion brought renewed claims in Quebec for breaking Ottawa's monopoly of the power of appointment of judges to the Supreme Court of Canada. There was suggested the creation of a special new constitutional court following general continental European, and especially West German, models.

The Montreal International Airport quarrel between the federal government and the province of Quebec arose in 1969 out of the need to make further long-range provisions for the handling of international air traffic to and from Montreal. Montreal was then Canada's major international airport and expansion was needed because of vastly increased air traffic and because of the anticipated era of jumbo jets and the supersonic passenger aircraft. Plans for extension of the existing international airport, Dorval, in the southwestern suburbs of Montreal had been abandoned, perhaps too quickly, on the basis of the noise factor.

The Province of Quebec then suggested a number of sites to the east of Montreal – either southeast, due east, or northeast of the city, but especially the south-eastern site. This easterly orientation best accorded with the projections made by the province's economic planning and research bureau on the future trends and directions of economic development in the province. For the province's economic advisers had concluded that the future economic development of the province lay along a Montreal-Quebec City axis – that is, along a ribbon of economic development running due east and north-east from Montreal towards Quebec city.

Pointing to the new rôle of the airport today as regional economic catalyst (as recognized particularly in the advanced airport location and planning science in the United States), the province pleaded for a site east of Montreal.

It cited also the enormous financial expenditures expected from the province for construction of airport access roads, urban development, and the like. The province asked the federal government to recognize a common federal-provincial interest in the choice to be made and suggested accordingly the formation of a federal-provincial committee to make a rational choice balancing the respective federal and provincial interests.

The federal government's response was categorical. Claiming a monopoly of constitutional power to decide where the new airport should be located, the federal government rejected the province's arguments and insisted on placing the new airport on a site north-west of Montreal. This site was away from the main projected axis of future economic development for the province and, in fact, in a diametrically opposed direction, towards Ontario. While direct, bilateral negotiations for formation of a joint federal-provincial committee were still going on between Quebec and federal Transport Minister Jamieson, Prime Minister Trudeau burnt his bridges. In a dramatic gesture, the Prime Minister flew in by helicopter to the federally favoured north-west site in order to deliver on the site itself a speech declaring the federal choice of the north-western site to be irrevocable.

The BNA Act of 1867 contains of course no direct allocation of the constitutional competence over airport location, air communication, aeronautics, or aviation generally. In the so-called *Aeronautics* case,[7] the Imperial Privy Council in 1932 had held that there was a constitutional power in the federal government to implement legislatively treaties entered into by the British government on behalf of Canada in the international aviation field. But this decision was based directly on the old 'British Empire' treaties section of the BNA Act (section 132), which the Privy Council, in the *Labour Conventions* case of 1937, later held to be legally defunct in view of the disappearance of the old empire and therefore of 'British Empire' treaties as such. The only other decision in any way relevant was a 1951 decision given by the Supreme Court of Canada concerning an airport zoning case involving municipal (town) delegated legislative authority. In this, the *Johannesson* case,[8] the Supreme Court, in denying the municipal (town) authority, had by implication decided in favour of the federal government's claims. The *Johannesson* rationale, however, was limited to very special facts and thus could very easily be distinguished from the facts of the Montreal International Airport quarrel, if the Supreme Court wanted to do so. In technical terms, its *ratio decidendi* was different.

The federal government, in the quarrel, relied upon its claimed 'general,' 'residual' legislative power under section 91. Quebec pointed to the newly accepted rôle of the modern airport as regional economic catalyst. Accordingly, it stressed those aspects of the choice of location having to do with regional economic planning, the provision of access roads and the like – all matters accepted to be within provincial constitutional competence under section 92. Quebec avoided the temptation of an extreme argument that, because of the new community acceptance of the importance of economic factors in airport site location and choice, the whole subject now fell within provincial powers and was therefore a *provincial* monopoly. The province contended, rather, that the subject was one of mixed, federal *and* provincial jurisdiction, with some aspects falling under federal power (air security matters) and others within provincial power (economic and urban planning).

In suggesting acceptance of such a new, mixed, federal-provincial jurisdiction to be exercised on a basis of mutual give-and-take and co-operation, the province necessarily sought to break away from the old 'watertight compartments' conception of the division of legislative powers.[9] By this old view, the BNA Act had established a constitutional dichotomy with matters being *either* exclusively federal *or* exclusively provincial, without the possibility of joint jurisdiction. In the absence of any federal-provincial consensus on the location of the proposed airport and of any disposition on either side to compromise or withdraw, the matter seemed headed for a constitutional testing before the Supreme Court.

Any such constitutional action was halted by the announcement of a provincial election in Quebec for April 1970, and by the defeat of the incumbent *Union nationale* government at those elections. The new Liberal government of Quebec accepted the federal Liberal government's designation of the site for the new airport. The basic question of division of powers was not so readily set aside.

5
Ottawa Stirs

The Quiet Revolution had begun to manifest itself in a series of specific Quebec proposals for institutional changes in the Canadian federal system. Any federal government initiatives in the constitutional law field could hardly avoid being labelled as purely defensive political measures, or at least as being no more than reactions to Quebec events. This labelling was, I think, somewhat unfair and innaccurate. The historical roots of various federal constitutional proposals of the late 1960s and early 1970s are to be found in the Pearson government's initiatives. These were often constructive, imaginative, and forward-looking for their time, given the difficulties under which a minority federal government must operate.

Immediately after the election of the first Pearson minority government in 1963, the Royal Commission on Bilingualism and Biculturalism was set up at the suggestion of the prominent French-Canadian intellectual and editor of *Le Devoir*, André Laurendeau. He became co-chairman of the commission and guided it until his untimely death before the commission had completed its work. Laurendeau was himself one of the intellectual progenitors of the Quiet Revolution and saw in the commission an instrument for strengthening and preserving French-Canadian language and culture through the application of existing federal constitutional powers.[1] The key consequence of the Laurendeau-Dunton Commission was the federal Official Languages Act of 1969.

The Pearson government began extensive constitutional negotiations with the provinces designed in the first place to secure self-operating amending machinery for the Canadian constitution. This particular choice seems to have been made for tactical reasons on the assumption (perhaps mistaken) that the subject was technical and therefore unlikely to arouse controversy between Ottawa and the provinces. The amending machinery was to be inserted in the BNA Act of 1867 and thus replace the elaborate existing system of combined conventional (customary) law and Imperial statute law. After extensive consultations with the provinces, and with their prior assent, the federal government used to approach the British government for a formal amendment by way of statute of the British Parliament. The whole subject had been discussed among the federal government and the provinces over almost half a century, and most recently had been taken up by John Diefenbaker's Justice Minister, Davie Fulton, and carried on by his successor in the Pearson ministry, Guy Favreau.[2] An informal consensus had been reached among the federal and provincial governments on a new amending formula – the so-called Fulton-Favreau formula. It, however, had lapsed when Jean Lesage later had to withdraw in the face of complaints that the new formula would introduce a new and unnecessary element of rigidity into the constitution before Quebec's aspirations had been effected. The federal response was to proceed over the next few years to try to assemble a package of constitutional proposals for the provinces, including amending machinery. Ottawa also proposed now an 'entrenched' bill of rights which was – as with the original Fulton-Favreau formula – assumed to be self-evident, demonstrably necessary, and free from federal-provincial conflict. This new package of federal constitutional proposals, if adopted by the provinces, involved consequent changes in the British North America Act, and came to be known as the Victoria Charter of 1971.

A final area of federal government activity – apart from the royal commission and inter-governmental negotiations – was the recourse to a special committee of enquiry of the federal Parliament. This was the Molgat-MacGuigan Committee with members from the Senate and House of Commons. Legislative committees of enquiry have not, in modern times, had any very great influence or prestige in Canada. This committee, however, had as its co-chairman one of the most able and thoughtful of the government back-benchers, Mark MacGuigan, and numbered among its rank-and-file members the independent and out-spoken Liberal member, Pierre DeBané.

The Official Languages Act, 1969, declares right at the outset that 'the English and French languages are the official languages of Canada for all purposes of the Parliament and Government of Canada, and possess and enjoy equality of status and equal rights and privileges as to their use in all the institutions of the Parliament and Government of Canada' (section 2).[3]

This provision does not significantly extend the stipulation in article 133 of the BNA Act that 'Either the English or the French Language may be used by any Person in the Debates of the Houses of the Parliament of Canada,' and that both languages may be used in the federal courts. The key modification, however, is in the status of 'official language' given to both English and French, and in the application of the status not merely to the federal Parliament but to the government of Canada generally. The act spells out that all statutory and other instruments directed to the public by the federal government and its agencies and federal courts are to be promulgated in both official languages (sections 3–7). Federal departments, agencies, courts, and Crown corporations are to provide services to the public in both official languages (sections 9–11); federal bilingual districts may be created (sections 12–18); and a Commissioner of Official Languages is to be appointed to oversee (with power of investigation) the application of the Official Languages Act (sections 19–34).

The sanctions attached to the act are not spelled out, and it is clear that its effective application depends upon the will of the federal government concerned and the enthusiasm and ability of the Commissioner to influence and control public opinion. The Supreme Court, in *Jones* v. *Attorney-General of Canada*,[4] upheld the constitutionality of the act against a challenge from a private taxpayer's suit. The challenge was based on the argument that section 133 of the BNA Act (with its specified limited federal categories of the federal legislature and the federal courts), in effect exhausted the field for affirmative federal government action in behalf of the French language.

The reach of the act is constitutionally limited to the federal government and its agencies. Yet, on both counts – the attitudes of the federal government and of the Commissioner – the new legislation had a good start in maximizing the use of the French language within the federal government.

There is a provision as to 'orderly adaptation to Act' (section 39) authorizing deferral or suspension of application of the act in cases where it would otherwise 'unduly prejudice the interests of the public' or 'be seriously detrimental to the good government of the authority, employer and employee relations or the effective management of its affairs' (sub-section 1). Nonetheless, the major complaints concerning the act alleged excessive zeal in its implementation and the cost of its application in situations where, it was suggested, public demand hardly existed for services in both languages. If the purpose of the act was to remedy the lack of recognition of the 'French fact' within the federal government, these criticisms suggest that the measure was achieving success – whatever problems it created in the process. The act focused upon the French fact and perhaps intentionally thereby increased the percentage of French-Canadians in the federal public service, particularly at the higher levels.

Ottawa submitted its 'Victoria Charter' proposals for constitutional change to the provincial governments at a working session in February 1971. They were then brought forward at a special federal-provincial constitutional conference held in Victoria, BC on 14-16 June 1971, and accepted in principle by the heads of government concerned.

Some of the proposals discussed at Victoria had been around a long time. No apparent consequences had resulted from the prolonged inaction upon them, and there had been little public concern over the delays. This was true of the proposed 'patriation' (or repatriation) of the BNA Act, in order that it would cease to be a statute of the British Parliament. The term 'patriation' was no more than a poetic designation of what had been presented to the provinces in the 'Fulton-Favreau formula.'

The emphasis at Victoria upon 'patriation' seems to have been a direct product of English-Canadian nationalism, and possibly stemmed from the assumption that this would please Quebec. There is no evidence, however, that French-Canadian nationalists, who have normally shown a keen sense of the difference between form and substance, were in any way concerned about the issue. As it was, all the attention to 'patriation' served to obscure a new and highly complicated constitutional amending machinery (Victoria Charter, articles 49–57). This would scrap the convention requiring consent of the federal government and all the provinces on matters of substance. The abandonment of the unanimity rule was noticed in Quebec – in the legislature (among the opposition forces), in the universities, and in the newspapers. This realization brought the charge, once again, that Quebec would be placing itself in a constitutional strait-jacket if it agreed to the Victoria Charter proposals (including, above all, the new 'patriation' proposals). Rather, Quebec had first to achieve acceptance by the federal government and the other provinces of its own proposals for substantive changes in the federal system. This reaction brought political embarrassment for Premier Bourassa, who had already agreed in principle to the package of constitutional changes. He finally had to renege upon his preliminary assent.

Beyond 'patriation,' the Victoria Charter proposals, except perhaps on 'language rights,' do not break much new ground. Does a reform proposal that reiterates the obvious or the already-existing justify a special constitutional conference? 'Modernisation of the Constitution' (articles 58–61, plus Schedule) provided for repeal of sections of the BNA Act that had fallen into disuse over the years, and for the renaming of certain other enactments, and would no doubt tidy up the constitution. In fact, however, as with most statutes, the obsolete sections had done no demonstrable harm. The part on 'Regional Disparities' (articles 46–7) is no more than a pious affirmation principle without any concrete constitutional engagement. Article 48 on 'Federal-Provincial Consultation' would only codify what already exists as a matter of practice.

The Supreme Court section, articles 22–42, would introduce a cumbersome system of federal-provincial consultation for federal appointments to the Supreme Court. This part of the charter is neither tidily nor elegantly drafted. What, for example, is the 'appropriate Province' (articles 26, 27, 28, 29) for federal-provincial agreement that is supposed to precede any filling of a vacancy on the Supreme Court? It seems clear from the language of the whole part that this goes beyond the three judges who come from Quebec (article 25). Does it mean that the federal government is now tacitly accepting the principle of designated, regionally 'representative' judges? These lengthy, detailed provisions would perhaps be more appropriately included in an ancillary statute than in a constitutional charter. They give the illusion of effective provincial participation in the appointment of Supreme Court judges without, however, changing the reality of federal power. It is the federal government alone that retains the right, under the proposed new system, to submit the names of proposed appointees (article 31). Similarly, by introducing a complex and rigid bureaucratic machinery for federal judicial appointments, the federal government would restrict its own discretionary power limiting itself to orthodox or non-controversial candidates. Would a Holmes or a Brandeis reach our Supreme Court under the proposed system of appointments? This particular portion of the charter starts out as a 'reform' but perhaps ends as worse than the existing arrangements.

That part of the charter having to do with 'Political Rights' (articles 1–9) includes freedom of thought, conscience and religion; freedom of opinion and expression; and freedom of peaceful assembly and of association' (article 1). The articles do not significantly extend political and civil rights. These were effectively established under John Diefenbaker's statutory Bill of Rights of 1960, and in the 'received' English common-law constitutional rights authoritatively recognized and declared by the Supreme Court in its existing case law. The part on 'Language Rights' (articles 10–19) ventures into language rights in the provinces, a subject on which a clear national consensus had not emerged. For Quebec, the reduction of 'language rights' to a neat constitutional formulation would be perhaps the end rather than the beginning of the solution of the problem, since a constitutional formulation would be dependent upon attainment of a prior political consensus in the province.

The Victoria Charter proposals fell when Premier Bourassa failed to secure acceptance for them when he returned to Quebec. They remained in reserve, however, as basic federal proposals for constitutional change in response to Quebec's challenges, and as a possible starting-point for any renewed round of negotiations.

The Special Joint Committee of the Senate and of the House of Commons had its genesis in resolutions of the House and Senate in January and February 1970. As a Parliamentary Joint Committee it had two co-chairmen, Senator Molgat and Mark MacGuigan, MP; and its membership was drawn from both houses and included representatives of the different political parties in Parliament. There were to be public hearings held throughout Canada with the general public invited to attend and offer opinions. Expert evidence on the constitution and its operation today was solicited by the committee from constitutional specialists of a wide range of political persuasions.

The mandate of the committee was formulated in very general terms, covering the whole field, including the abortive Victoria Charter proposals. The most controversial aspects of the final report had to do with the fundamental philosophy of the constitution, including the issue of national self-determination.[5] This part of the report attracted a dissenting or minority report from two committee members, Pierre DeBané, MP (Liberal), and Martial Asselin, MP (Progressive Conservative). The rest of the report ranged over federal institutions (including the Head of State, Senate, House of Commons, and Supreme Court); division of legislative powers between the federal government and the provinces; fundamental rights; and language rights.

The committee recommended no changes in the existing arrangements for the federal Head of State (a Governor-General representing the monarch), saying that any formal alteration would be a 'highly emotional issue.' It took note of the evolutionary process in which, by developing constitutional convention, the Governor-General had in effect become Head of State of Canada (recommendations 33, 34).

The committee recommended that the positive-law right of the Senate, under the BNA Act of 1867, to apply a full veto over legislation adopted by the House of Commons, be reduced to a six-month suspensive veto. Since the full veto power of the Senate had in practice atrophied, this provision would simply bring constitutional law into line with long-time constitutional practice (recommendation 35). While all Senators should continue to be appointed by the federal government, there was a provision that, as vacancies occurred in the present Senate, one half of the senators from each province and territory should be 'appointed by the federal Government from a panel of nominees submitted by the appropriate Provincial or Territorial Government' (recommendation 39). There was also provision for changes in the geographical and regional distribution of senators, the main effect being to increase substantially representation from the western provinces (recommendation 38).

The recommendations on the House of Commons focused largely upon the issue of a fixed, four-year term for Parliament, subject only to an executive right of dissolution in the case of a 'no confidence' vote and to the House of Commons' own right to adopt a resolution requesting dissolution (recommendation 43). This proposal was directed towards 'lessening the control of the executive over the legislative branch of government.'

On the Supreme Court of Canada, the committee did not differ much from the Victoria Charter on federal-provincial consultation on court appointments. It did, however, suggest that the provinces – in addition to the federal government – have the right to submit nominations to the federal-provincial nominating committees envisaged under the Victoria Charter (recommendation 45). It also recommended that the provinces have the right to withdraw appeals in matters of strictly provincial law from the Supreme Court of Canada and to vest final decision in such matters in their own provincial courts (recommendation 46).

The committee, courageously for its time, ventured into the constitutional division of powers between the federal government and the provinces – sections 91 and 92 of the BNA Act. The committee recognized that the balance between federal and provincial powers had fluctuated considerably under the Privy Council's interpretation of the BNA Act. It was – perhaps understandably for a federal committee – somewhat critical of the Watson-Haldane rôle in producing a more decentralized, provincially oriented constitution – 'much too extreme' in the committee's view. When it came to making actual recommendations for change in the existing division of legislative powers, the committee was somewhat general and unspecific. This presumably reflected the difficulty of obtaining consensus within a multi-party group. It recommended maintenance of exclusive lists of federal and provincial powers, but with an extended list of concurrent powers (recommendation 49).

On the difficult issue of legislative paramountcy in federal-provincial conflicts over concurrent powers, the committee specified that 'concurrent powers which predominantly affect the national interest should grant paramountcy to the federal Parliament and those which predominantly affect Provincial or local interests should grant paramountcy to the Provincial legislatures.' It did not, however, offer clear and objective criteria to decide whether a concurrent power affects the 'national' interest or 'Provincial or local' interests (recommendation 50). This, however, is surely the key question, and would presumably, under the existing arrangements, go to the Supreme Court for decision.

There is thus little if any advance on the present system of division of powers. The committee at the same time rejected the concession to any province of legislative power over certain subjects for which the federal government would generally have legislative power for the remaining provinces. It argued that this would amount to 'special status' which, it seemed to conclude, would be unsound. 'Special constitutional provisions for one or several provinces' it evidently found acceptable, and it cited, as an example, Quebec's power to legislate concerning its own *droit civil*.

On taxing powers the committee recommended that Ottawa and the provinces have access to all fields of taxation, with provision for federal-provincial 'consultations to determine the most equitable means of apportioning joint fields of taxation' (recommendation 54). The provinces should have the right to impose 'indirect' taxes, 'provided that they do not impede interprovincial or international trade and do not fall on persons resident in other Provinces' (recommendation 55).

The federal 'spending power,' in the view of some critics, has been the principal instrument for expansion of federal power at the expense of the provinces. The committee proposed a complex system of inter-governmental controls to prevent any federal abuses in the future. The power of the federal government to make conditional grants for federal-provincial (shared-cost) programs should henceforth be 'subject to the establishment of a national consensus both for the institution of any new programme and for the continuation of any existing one.' This 'consensus' was to be evidenced by the affirmative vote of the provincial legislatures in three of the four regions of Canada (the Atlantic provinces, Quebec, Ontario, and the West) (recommendation 56). Moreover, if a province did not wish to participate in a program for which there was such a 'national consensus,' the federal government should pay the provincial government concerned a 'sum equal to the amount it would have cost the federal government to implement the program in the Province' (recommendation 57).

There had been widespread provincial criticism of the Supreme Court of Canada's Advisory Opinion on the *Off-shore Mineral Rights* question[6] (see chapter 4). The Joint Committee reacted defensively by affirming that Ottawa ought to have proprietary rights over the seabed off-shore and full legislative jurisdiction over it. Further, there should be no constitutional provision for the sharing of profits from the exploitation of seabed resources (recommendations 72 and 73). The committee indicated, however, that it felt 'strongly' that the federal government should 'share the profits of seabed development equally with the adjacent coastal Province rather than with all of the Provinces' (recommendation 73).

Finally, on international relations, the committee recommended outright repeal of section 132 of the BNA Act. This had been the source of the 1937 Privy Council ruling on the *Labour Conventions* affair[7] (see chapter 4). According to that decision the federal government could not, simply by making a treaty on a particular subject, obtain legislative jurisdiction over that subject if it would, in the absence of the treaty, be within provincial legislative powers under the BNA Act. In recommending exclusive jurisdiction for the federal government over 'foreign policy, the making of treaties,' the committee offered several gestures to the provinces. These included an obligation on the federal government to 'consult' with any province affected by a treaty obligation, prior to the federal government's binding itself to perform such treaty obligation; the right of a province to 'remain free not to take any action with respect to an obligation undertaken by the Government of Canada under a treaty unless it has agreed to do so'; and the right of a province, 'subject to a veto power in the Government of Canada ... to enter into contracts, and administrative, reciprocal and other arrangements with foreign states' (recommendations 75–6, 78–9, 80).

The report would institutionalize the existing informal federal-provincial premiers' conferences by an express requirement that they be called at least once a year. It called for the creation of federal ministry of Intergovernmental Affairs and a permanent federal-provincial secretariat (recommendations 60–2). The committee also followed the Victoria Charter proposals for a constitutionally entrenched bill of rights. Such a bill would be approximately coterminuous with the 1960 Bill of Rights and those common-law constitutional rights already recognized in Supreme Court decisions (recommendations 13–21).

The committee also touched on language rights, indicating 'support for the general objective of making French the working language in Quebec ... with due respect for certain Quebec Anglophonic institutions, and taking into account the North American and world reality' (recommendation 26). It suggested that the constitution should 'recognise parents' rights to have English or French provided as their child's main language of instruction in publicly supported schools in areas where the language of their choice is chosen by a sufficient number of persons to justify the provision of the necessary facilities' (recommendation 25). These committee proposals were advanced *before* the report of Quebec's own Royal Commission on the French Language and Language Rights in Quebec (Commission Gendron).

Understandably, they are somewhat unspecific on competing federal-provincial, and particularly Ottawa-Quebec, jurisdictional claims and policies in the language field.

The most controversial, and perhaps the most *avant-garde* proposal concerned 'Self-Determination.' The actual recommendation (number 6) is rather modest in its choice of language. The preamble to the constitution should recognize that 'the existence of Canadian society rests on the free consent of its citizens and their collective will to live together, and that any differences among them should be settled by peaceful means.' The report nevertheless states in its supporting argumentation that it 'would rather be appropriate to recognize self-determination as a right belonging to people,' and it cites the UN Charter in support of this position. It also expressly rejects the 'use of military or other coercive force' to resolve any federal conflict with any province over continuation of the present political system (recommendation 7).

Two members of the committee, Pierre DeBané (Liberal) and Martial Asselin (Progressive Conservative), filed a minority report directed expressly to the question of the right of self-determination. The co-chairman, Mark MacGuigan, and the federal government invoked British parliamentary practice as justification for not joining this minority report to the committee's final report in its official publication.[8] The joint dissent argued the necessity for an 'authentic' constitutional revision, starting with their proposal that the preamble of the constitution recognize explicitly the existence and the aspirations of Quebec society. It asked that the constitution contain an express recognition of Quebec's fundamental right to self-determination. It touched on the division of powers, and postulated as fundamental the principle that the federal government should have jurisdiction only in the areas expressly reserved to it. In other words, the residual powers should belong to the provinces and the latter ought to consent explicitly to every proposed enlargement of the sphere of federal competence.

These were Ottawa's major constitutional activities in the early Trudeau years. The Official Languages Act, the Victoria Charter proposals and the Molgat-MacGuigan Committee Report reflected Ottawa's official willingness at least to consider changes in the constitution and, among other things, to utilize a linguistic analysis of Canada's problems as a means of reconciling her two peoples. The attitude towards a linguistic approach of the province most concerned – Quebec – may perhaps be seen in its own language legislation.

6
Quebec Acts: Bills 22 and 101

Since the inauguration of the Quiet Revolution at the opening of the 1960s, Quebec society has been transformed by rapid and fundamental social and economic changes. There have been the rapid and large-scale industrialization and urbanization of a conservative rural and agrarian society. The conflict with traditional values and traditional institutions like the family has been represented by the growing anti-clerical movement. An emerging French-Canadian middle class has begun to challenge the erstwhile dominance by 'Anglo-Saxon' (English-speaking) interests of Quebec commercial and economic life. These events have by now entered the stage of historical folklore, summed up in the very title of the 'Quiet Revolution.' As an innovator and reformer Jean Lesage moved rather too quickly for a society that still contained within itself formidable pockets of resistance to change. Lesage, who is usually associated with the era of the Quiet Revolution, was defeated in the provincial elections of 1966. The successor, *Union nationale* (conservative) government, led first by Daniel Johnson and later by Jean-Jacques Bertrand, did not attempt to reverse the course of the Quiet Revolution. But the *Union nationale* ministry, nevertheless, meant a period of comparative governmental *attente*. The *Union nationale* contained within itself two sharply conflicting wings – the older, conservative and traditional groups, and the younger, radical and nationalist elements. The late sixties saw the explosion of French-Canadian nationalist sentiments in the attempt to maintain and extend the use of the French language as a symbol of the new nationalism. Public life, industry, and, most immediately and controversially, the government-financed public schools of the province were affected. The Bertrand government was unwilling or unable to elaborate a language policy in tune with these rising nationalist sentiments. It adopted the time-hallowed Canadian expedient – appointment of a royal commission to conduct a judicial enquiry into the language problem and to recommend legislative solutions to the government. The Gendron Royal Commission was named in late 1968, and presented its official report to the government on 31 December 1972.

In the meantime, the Bertrand government had been defeated in the provincial election of April 1970. It was replaced by a Liberal government headed by Jean Lesage's successor as party leader, Robert Bourassa. The Bourassa government seemed to promise a revival of the reformist, modernizing drive of the earlier Quiet Revolution era. Many members of the new government, including the new premier himself, were young and had impressive academic or professional qualifications or significant commercial and industrial experience.

The Bourassa government responded to the increasing pressures for French-Canadian self-determination by offering new legislation to give a much greater rôle than before to the French language in Quebec. After securing a more substantial mandate in the provincial election specially called in 1973, Premier Bourassa proceeded essentially to adopt the recommendations of the Gendron Commission in special legislation enacted in 1974 that became known as Bill 22. Affirmative action on the protection and extension of the French language might seem to threaten the special interests or privileges not merely of the economically powerful, 'Anglo-Saxon,' English-speaking minority in Quebec, but also of various immigrant groups. These were originally neither English-speaking nor French-speaking, but had chosen English as their language of work and hence as their first language in Quebec.

Premier Bourassa attempted ingeniously, but, in the end vainly, to reconcile these conflicting political interests in one piece of legislation. Bill 22 went beyond the Gendron Commission recommendations by legislating in the field of education and the schools. However, the bill had built into it legal standards that would allow administrators considerable leeway in actual application of the bill. These concessions – both to French-Canadian and to 'Anglo-Saxon' and 'immigrant' interests – satisfied no one. Bourassa expected re-election and sought a fresh mandate for negotiating with Ottawa greater decentralization in favour of Quebec's special claims. He therefore called a general election for November 1976. His government was deserted both by the 'Anglo-Saxon' and 'immigrant' voters and also by the more advanced French-Canadian nationalist elements and was replaced by a *Parti québécois* Government headed by René Lévesque. Lévesque had been a member of the Lesage government that had begun the Quiet Revolution in the early 1960s. The Lévesque government's general electoral program, somewhat along European Social Democratic lines, undoubtedly contributed to its victory in 1976; but the language issue was nevertheless decisive then. The new premier promised to introduce before the next election a public referendum on the issue of the secession of Quebec from the Canadian federal system. At the same time he announced legislation intended to strengthen and extend the French language in Quebec, in replacement of the former government's Bill 22.

The Royal Commission on the French Language and Language Rights in Quebec (Commission Gendron) was first appointed by the Bertrand government in December 1968. It came in the aftermath of the civic conflict over the attempt of the school board in St Léonard, a suburb of Montreal, to direct the children of Italian immigrant families to French-language schools. The commission was given a mandate specified in essentially 'linguistic' terms. Yet the commission was soon caught in the middle of the more general crisis of the middle and late 1960s. The wide gap between the ideals and high hopes of the Quiet Revolution and the practical possibilities for translating those goals into action had become apparent.

The political and economic *malaise* of Quebec society was reflected in the plethora of competing interests and demands presented by the various community pressure groups appearing before the commission, either by written brief or in person. Some of these interest groups sought the recognition of the principle of national self-determination which seemed to them to mean separation from the rest of Canada. Other groups conceived the problem as one of power. They saw an essentially tired and effete 'Anglo-Saxon' economic 'establishment' in Quebec that was unable or unwilling to adapt to the demands of the rapidly rising French-Canadian middle class. The latter desired greater and more effective participation in the key economic and commercial decisions in Quebec more or less in proportion to the percentage of the French-Canadians in the total population of Quebec. The proponents of national self-determination sought some sort of 'political' revolution or break-away for Quebec. Those who contended for economic power were arguing for an even more profound and far-reaching economic revolution. They sought the replacement of one economic élite by a new and younger French one. These were the two most striking claims presented before the commission, but by no means the only ones. For there were pleas to halt a growing 'Anglicization' or 'Americanization' or 'vulgarization' of the French language and culture. Many French-Canadians in lower-income groups feared that their prospects for advancement and promotion, and even their job security, were jeopardized by the predominance of the English language in commerce and industry, both in Quebec and in North America as a whole.

The commission was able to identify the following as the key factors conditioning and controlling its ultimate recommendations:

(i) The historically-demonstrated inferiority of the French-Canadian, on the economic plane, in Quebec;

(ii) The essentially rather negative conception historically taken by the English-speaking economic *élite* in Quebec of the French-Canadians' claim to equality of opportunity in the direction of the industrial and economic development of Quebec;

(iii) The obligation effectively falling upon French-Canadians working in industry to possess a knowledge, more or less advanced, of English, whether for external communications with their own company's head offices, with competitors, with clients or customers, with suppliers, or whether for technical or instructional communications; and all this even in situations where the claim is advanced that French is the language of internal communications in those establishments;

(iv) The propensity of immigrants to opt (either for themselves or for their children) for the English language as language of usage in Quebec;

(v) The minimal utility that the French language has historically had for English-speaking Quebecers, a fact which manifests itself in the minimal motivation that English-speaking Quebecers have historically manifested for learning French;

(vi) The comparative failure of institutions of advanced learning in Quebec, whether universities or technical institutes, to develop a technologically sophisticated managerial skill group of sufficient numbers among the French-Canadian population.[1]

The Gendron Commission's Report, finally presented to the Quebec government on 31 December 1972, ran to three volumes of 1,423 pages.[2] There were also detailed supporting studies, published separately from the main report, in excess of 10,000 pages.

In sum, the commission's report amounted to a sophisticated series of recommendations, emphasizing at all times the constitutionally possible.[3] This overriding concern for constitutional competence was reflected in the first main recommendation concerning an official language for Quebec. It did not in any way try to derogate from the provisions of section 133 of the BNA Act of 1867 which, in effect, establishes French and English as two *federal* public languages in Quebec. The commission suggested the Quebec government should legislate forthwith to proclaim French the official language of the province of Quebec. Such a proclamation would fall wholly within the competence of the province of Quebec. It would mean that the French character of the public activities of the province and its institutions would be officially recognized. Such a proclamation would not have any legal implications for private activities within the province. It would be a declaration of a largely spiritual quality, recognizing symbolically the best French-Canadian nationalist aspirations of the Quiet Revolution.

The commission also recommended formal recognition of a certain preferred status for English within the province, corresponding to the various statutorily based privileges concerning its use in education and elsewhere. The commission's ancillary recommendation was that English be recognized with French as a national language of Quebec. While French would become the sole official language, English would also be recognized as a language deserving limited public protection within the province of Quebec.

In its second recommendation the commission moved directly from the symbolic to the concrete, namely to commerce and industry and the work milieu in general, its main field for community action. It drew very fully upon the lessons of sociological jurisprudence as to the limited effectiveness of coercive measures. It accordingly recommended that the government proceed by legislation, administrative decrees and practice, and by voluntary, persuasive measures – 'to make French a language that is useful and necessary in communications within all fields of activity in commerce and industry and the work *milieu* in general, in the Province of Quebec.'

The commission indicated that the governmental intervention here recommended was 'designed to ensure, in a pragmatic, empirical way, that French is established as the *language of Internal Communication in commerce and industry and the work milieu in general*, in the Province of Quebec, and ultimately as the common language of all Quebecers.'

As a corollary the commission also advised that, in the same 'pragmatic, empirical way,' the government should 'endeavour, by voluntary, persuasive or facultative, community measures, to ensure far greater vertical mobility on the part of French-Canadians in commerce and industry operating in the Province of Quebec.'[4]

In particular, the commission suggested the government should try by these methods to 'ensure far greater access by French-Canadians to "command" or decision-making posts in commerce and industry operating in the Province of Quebec, having a general regard, though certainly not in any rigid or mechanical way, to the relative proportions of French-Canadians' in the population of the province of Quebec.

The last group of recommendations of the commission was a consequence of the deliberate priority chosen by the commission for commerce and industry and the work milieu in general. It recognized that the province did not possess unlimited resources for community problem-solving, and that it must therefore marshal its resources in the most useful way. The Commission therefore recommended a moratorium on community intervention in the two particular areas where group passions and prejudices could be expected to run highest. Here the outpouring of public emotion could be expected to militate against the effectiveness of community problem-solving energies. The commission therefore recommended that, notwithstanding its full competence, the government take no action in the areas of public education in Quebec or of immigrants to Canada taking up residence in Quebec. This moratorium should last for three to five years – a 'cooling-off' period.

The main French-Canadian nationalist complaint in this area had been that the public education system in Quebec, supported and financed by the provincial government, was being misused, thereby accentuating and accelerating the decline of the French language. Immigrant groups settling in Quebec generally enrolled their children in English-language schools even when they came from French-speaking or predominantly Latin and Roman Catholic countries.

The French-Canadian nationalist view presented to the commission was that immigrants to Quebec from non-English-speaking countries should be required to enrol their children in French-language schools. If these immigrants did not want to place their children in the French-language schools, they could always settle in some other province. Indeed they could, for that matter, immigrate to some country other than Canada. The commission disposed of some of the more extreme legal arguments – for example, the claim that an immigrant settling in Quebec had an 'acquired' or 'Natural Right' to have his children educated in the public schools in any language that he might choose.

The commission still recommended making an ally of time in order to see whether the recommended community interventions in commerce and industry and the work milieu would be successful. The commission was also influenced by the principle of economy in the use of power. It did not want to expend community resources in too many areas at the same time, fearing unnecessary dispersal of energies.

The commission took note of the occasional recourse by extremist groups to direct action outside the normal political processes. It recommended strengthening and improving the system of political representation in the province to ensure that all substantial political opinion within Quebec be directly represented in the legislature. No group would then have an excuse for taking grievances into the streets for settlement by direct action. The commission recommended that the government study the merits of proportional representation (total or partial) as a means of ensuring fuller and more effective political expression of minority group interests in Quebec.

Bill 22 was the Bourassa government's response to the Gendron Report. The report had been greeted with hostile and occasionally intemperate criticism from activist elements in both language groups in Quebec. The vanguard French-Canadian nationalist elements felt it had no teeth and did nothing to solve the crisis of the French language in Quebec. They saw the report as a surrender to the Anglo-Saxon establishment in Quebec. On the other hand, 'ultramontane' elements within the English-speaking community – what the federal government's Language Commissioner, Keith Spicer, later characterized as the 'Rhodesians' – bitterly attacked the commission for allegedly surrendering to the French-Canadian nationalists.

Granted such mutually irreconcilable criticisms, it might seem that the commission had in fact struck a reasonable balance between the differing group interests pressed before it. This was the apparent reaction of the Quebec government to the report. Its own legislative response to the language issue followed very closely the first two main recommendations and departed significantly from the commission's general philosophy only in the third main area – education.

The Quebec government waited well over a year after receiving the report, and, incidentally, obtained a new and stronger mandate in a general election in 1973, before announcing its language program in the spring of 1974. The package of language measures – Bill 22, which became the Official Language Act – was finally passed by the legislature and promulgated as law on 31 July 1974.[5]

The Quebec government adopted the commission's recommendation that French be made the official language of Quebec. The government's approach, in accordance with the commission's prescriptions, was deliberately limited to the area of provincial constitutional competence under sections 91 and 92 of the BNA Act. The government eschewed the suggestion of certain nationalist groups that it repeal section 133, which authorizes the use of English and French equally in the National Assembly and Quebec courts. They refused to repeal the section even though constitutional experts had told the commission that the province had full constitutional competence to do so.

On language of work the government accepted virtually *in toto* the philosophy and recommendations of the commission. The overriding emphasis was upon what the commission called 'friendly persuasion,' rather than on coercive or criminal-law measures. The implementation of 'friendly persuasion' meant inevitably, in the government's view, the use of general standards or guide-lines. These would allow the greatest possible flexibility to the administrator and avoid unnecessary rigidities or harshness in the application of the new language program. The flexible standards of the administrator thus tended to replace the precise legal categories of the lawyer. The government undoubtedly profited from the new wave of thinking in continental European *droit administratif*, to which young French-Canadian lawyers and administrators had been exposed during their post-graduate training in France after the Quiet Revolution. This approach did, however, cause some confusion and some fear on the part of English-speaking lawyers, used to more traditional English administrative-law formulae and processes. It also raised the question whether the sophisticated approach of contemporary French *droit administratif* is not predicated upon the existence of the special administrative review and control system institutionalized in that brilliant, specialized and expert administrative court, the *Conseil d'Etat*.

On language of education, however, the government departed from the thrust of the commission's recommendations. These had counselled delay, until the measures recommended in the priority areas of official language and language of work were demonstrated to be ineffective. The review period recommended by the commission had been three to five years.

The government's decision to act on language of education[6] was predicated on significant changes in Quebec society between the time of formal submission of the report to the government in December 1972 and the introduction of Bill 22 in the spring of 1974. There was a further deterioration in the French situation in Quebec during that time, curtailing the three to five year 'cooling-off' period suggested by the commission. The substance of the government's new policy on education was to be found in chapter V (Language of Instruction) sections 40 to 44 of Bill 22 and in the express repeal (under section 112) of the so-called Bill 63 – a 1969 act to promote the French language in Quebec.[7] Bill 63 had been introduced by the Bertrand government in response to the St Léonard 'immigrants' conflict, as a stopgap measure pending completion of the Gendron Commission enquiry. It had conferred on parents the privilege of asking for and obtaining education in the English language for their children, even if English was not the maternal language of the children.

Article 40 of Bill 22 established the general principle that the language of instruction in Quebec public schools should be French, though it stipulated continuance of instruction in English. The balance between these two provisions was provided by the remaining provisions of chapter V. The apparent inadequacies in the conception and drafting of chapter V arose from compromises within the cabinet and from the attempt to reconcile two rather different, even conflicting approaches to securing and protecting the French language in education.[8]

Thus the third paragraph of article 40 seems to determine the language of instruction for any pupil by the mother tongue, whether French or English, of the pupil. It made any school board's decision to commence, cease, increase, or reduce instruction in English dependent upon the prior authorization of the Minister of Education. Such approval was not to be given unless the minister considered that the number of pupils whose mother tongue was English so warranted. Yet articles 41 to 43 seemed to establish a different language policy, namely linguistic competence. They set sufficient knowledge of the language of instruction as a pre-condition to a pupil's receiving instruction in English and set up a system of language tests to determine and apply that condition.

The first implementation of chapter v of Bill 22 occurred with the opening of the new Quebec school year in the autumn of 1975. There thus appeared the danger of fresh community conflicts over the language issue, when many immigrant families, whose maternal language was not English, attempted to evade the spirit if not the letter of chapter v of Bill 22. They sought to enrol their children in English-language schools, through the claim that their children had a sufficient knowledge of English. There thus appeared two seemingly different language policies – the *numerus clausus* philosophy of section 40 (3) and the language-competence emphasis of articles 41 to 43.

The Quebec government reacted quite flexibly in the autumn of 1975. It accepted at face value the professions of language-competence advanced by immigrant parents on behalf of their children and thereby permitted the transfer, in the not unduly large number of cases involved, into the English-language system. It thus seemed clear that under the Bourassa government policies pragmatism, not confrontation, was to be the key to implementation of the new French-language program. Such an approach was in keeping with the standards-orientation of the French *droit administratif* already mentioned.

This moderate approach had clearly assisted the federal government in its consistent decision to resist political pressures from English-language extremists within the Liberal party. These had sought federal intervention against Bill 22 by constitutional disallowance or reference to the Supreme Court of Canada for an advisory opinion as to its constitutionality. The political opponents of Bill 22 had unsuccessfully importuned the federal government to act against the bill. However, they all – and the Premier of New Brunswick was simply the most notable example[9] – lacked a valid constitutional 'interest' in their own right beyond that of any taxpayer, sufficient to challenge the Quebec government's program. Beyond this, the Quebec government's language program, in application and formulation, stayed determinedly and strictly within provincial legislative competence under the BNA Act. In giving French a special, preferred status within Quebec, Bill 22 in effect gave Quebec something of a special status in its own right; but this was perhaps no different in principle from the special status of English in the other nine provinces of Canada.

Bill 22 did not remain unchallenged. In 1976 Chief Judge Jules Deschênes of the Superior Court of Montreal gave judgment upon an action brought by the Protestant School Board of Greater Montreal[10] challenging the constitutionality of the new law. Judge Deschênes reaffirmed the elementary truth that article 93 of the BNA Act of 1867 is concerned with *religious* rights and has nothing to say about *language*. The terms of article 93 are clear and unambiguous. There is absolutely no room, under the ordinary English rules of constitutional construction applied by the Privy Council and the Canadian Supreme Court, for considering the intentions of the fathers of Canadian Confederation. This would be true even if their original intentions could be agreed upon by contemporary historians and rendered explicit.

Judge Deschênes first disposed rather easily of the Protestant School Board's case based upon claimed ambiguities or imprecisions in the text of article 93 itself. He made an extended *tour de force* survey of the historical origins of article 93 – case law from various provinces and the pre-Confederation school legislation of both Upper and Lower Canada. He also examined the assertion – unusual for an Anglo-Saxon pressure group like the Protestant School Board – of Natural Law rights operating to override and repeal both constitutional and statute law in the event of any inconsistency.

Rather than helping the Protestant School Board, this extraneous material, even if properly admissible, would simply have operated further to refute and defeat their cause. For there is absolutely nothing in the historical origins of article 93 supporting any linguistic import for its provisions. The case law on article 93, especially from the English-speaking provinces, gives no warrant for the assertion that the article protects linguistic rights. Rather, it revives for contemporary students rather sad memories of past intolerance by English-speaking Protestant majorities directed against the English-speaking provinces' own French-speaking Roman Catholic minorities. The argument that the pre-Confederation legislation of Lower Canada somehow guaranteed or entrenched certain vested language rights in the present-day Protestant schools in Quebec was demonstrated by Judge Deschênes as a purely fanciful creation lacking any serious historical foundation. Finally, the appeal to a rather vague Natural Law was disposed of by the Privy Council's own cool reminder, in the *Mackell* case in 1917:[11] invocations of claimed Natural Law rights in the context of article 93, however emotional their appeal, can only be recognized in so far as those rights should have been directly incorporated into the BNA Act itself. This is good sober 'Anglo-Saxon' common law jurisprudence. It is ironic that a French-Canadian civil law jurist was called upon to remind the English Protestant School Board of it.

There were several secondary arguments in the board's brief that were also quickly dismissed. It was contended, for example, that section 1 of Bill 22, in proclaiming French as the official language of Quebec, was in conflict with the federal Official Languages Act of 1969, and therefore with article 91 (1) of the BNA Act and its definition of federal law-making competence. It was also claimed that article 1 of Bill 22 interfered with the office of Lieutenant-Governor of the province as specifically protected by article 92 (1) of the BNA Act. But article 1 of Bill 22 was carefully drafted to extend only to provincial constitutional competence, thereby permitting 'peaceful coexistence' with the federal bilingual policies which were directed only to federal constitutional competence. Section 1 of Bill 22 had nothing at all to say about the office of Lieutenant-Governor.

A further contention was that section 2 of Bill 22, in providing for the primacy of the French text of Quebec laws in case of conflicts between the French and English texts that could not be resolved by the ordinary rules of interpretation, conflicted with article 133 of the BNA Act. The latter specifically provides for the printing and publishing of federal and Quebec laws in both French and English. The argument was refuted by simple comparison of the texts of section 2 of Bill 22 and of article 133 of the BNA Act. Section 2 established a modest rule of statutory interpretation to aid the courts in cases of ambiguity that could not be resolved by comparison of the French and English texts of a Quebec law taken together. Here, as with the final contention that Bill 22 was in conflict with the federal immigration laws and entered upon a domain of exclusive federal legislative competence – namely, legislation in relation to immigration – examination of the words of Bill 22 itself was sufficient to throw the argument out of court.

The question remained, once the substantive constitutional law arguments of the Protestant School Board had been so completely disposed of by the court, how such a constitutional case could ever have managed to go so far in the first place. Certainly the Quebec government, in its rejoinder to the Protestant School Board, raised the adjectival, procedural law issue of the school board's constitutional 'interest' to contest Bill 22. Judge Deschênes himself seems to have concluded that there might be a public interest in allowing the Protestant School Board members to be heard on the substance of the litigation, however remote their own personal connections thereto. It is also true, as the judge noted, that the current trend in Canadian Supreme Court jurisprudence – *Thorson*[12] in 1974, and *McNeil*[13] in 1975 – is towards following American trends towards enlarging and facilitating access to the courts by disaffected individuals, special interest associations, or political pressure groups.

But the Protestant School Board is a creation of the provincial government and, not less than other provincial government instrumentalities, might be said to owe respect for the law as duly enacted by the provincial legislature – and respect for the spirit as well as the letter of that law. There is a logical contradiction inherent in the notion that an agency such as the school board, itself partaking in measure of state (provincial) sovereignty, may appear in court in its own right to challenge the sovereign (provincial) legislature. For that matter the Attorney-General of Canada, as the ultimate defender of state sovereignty at the federal level, positively declined all invitations to participate in the argument before the court in the case, or even to be represented in the case.

The arguments as to alleged Bill 22 violations of federal sovereignty and of federal law-making competence under the BNA Act, or of alleged conflicts of Bill 22 with federal laws, came in no way from the federal government. They came rather from an agency – the Protestant School Board – that derived its legal personality and public financing from provincial legislative authority and that was affected, solely, with the provincial public interest. Issues of potential conflict of interest in the exercise of public office at the provincial level come readily to mind. Further, there are the older British and Commonwealth precedents which limit the use of the courts for guerilla-style warfare against the popularly elected organs of government. Are these precedents perhaps more applicable to Canada today than the more open-ended American case law on constitutional 'interest' and standing to sue?

Be that as it may, the judgment by Judge Deschênes bears all the evidence of a landmark decision in Quebec and Canadian constitutional history. In its legal aspects, the Judge's opinion is a model of Anglo-Saxon constitutional construction – a classical exercise in that logical and analytical approach to interpretation of the BNA Act first developed by the Imperial Privy Council and then carried on by the Canadian Supreme Court after 1949. Lords Watson and Haldane, in the golden era of Privy Council interpretation, would have needed to say no more than Judge Deschênes and would certainly have said no less.

Going beyond the narrower constitutional and legal issues, however, the judge tried to describe the sociological state of Canadian federalism. He presented the case for constitutional rewriting demanded by the change in society and its expectations since 1867, when the British North America Act was originally formulated.

The Treaty of Paris in 1763 formally ended the Seven Years' War in Europe and, incidentally, transferred sovereignty over Quebec from France to Great Britain. Judge Deschênes pointed out that what French-Canadian historians have blushingly qualified as cession, English-Canadian historians have more realistically – and strengthened by armed power – called conquest. In the struggle between these two rival conceptions of Canadian history that the two nations – French and English – have carried on for two centuries, Quebec's Bill 22, in the Chief Judge's view, constituted only one more episode. The battle had simply been transferred from the Plains of Abraham to the Quebec National Assembly and from there to the Halls of Justice, but the stakes had not changed.

As Judge Deschênes pointed out, we live at a major turning point in the history of Canada and of Quebec, when there are no longer victors and vanquished, or conquerors and conquered, but only two peoples called upon by an accident of history to share permanently the same corner of America. In this sense, the BNA Act of 1867 reflected the climate of its own times and contained conceptions which no longer reflected the reality of 1976.

In 1977 the newly elected PQ government of René Lévesque introduced a more comprehensive language law – Bill 101. In fulfilment of its promises in the 1976 campaign, the new government introduced into the *Assemblée nationale* on 1 April 1977 a White Paper[14] outlining the basis of the new law to replace Bill 22.

In résumé, the White Paper, except on education and schools, did not depart substantially from the philosophy or stipulations of Bill 22. It might indeed be contended that the Lévesque government language philosophy and policy were similar to what those of the Bourassa government might have been if it had not been defeated in 1976. The latter might have sponsored its own amendments to Bill 22, based on its analysis of the application of the bill during its first two or three years of operation. According to the Lévesque White Paper, there was now to be a further intensification of the 'French' character of the Quebec polity and its juridical manifestations. Laws would be adopted and promulgated only in French; the judgments rendered by Quebec courts would be in French with the French text as the sole authentic version. Further, the documentation published by the public administration would be in French and a commission would be created to render in French the names of places.

It was in education and schools that the White Paper presented the clearest break with the language policy of its predecessor, Bill 22. The test of a sufficient knowledge of English as a legal criterion for admission to an English-language public school, even on the part of a child whose parents were not English-speaking, was to be replaced by that of the maternal language of the parents. With certain limited and temporary exceptions, only children, at least one of whose parents has gone to an English-language primary school, would be admitted to English-language public schools in the future. The intention seems clear: all children of immigrant parents in Quebec should henceforth go to French-language schools, thus removing the major legal loophole in the education chapter of Bill 22. Large-scale flights had taken place by the children of non-English-speaking immigrants to the provincially supported English-language schools in Quebec. This legal loophole had been the result of a split among members of the Bourassa government at the time of the drafting of the bill. The resulting cabinet division had been papered over in a rather unsatisfactory verbal compromise in the text of the bill itself. Seemingly mutually incompatible principles had conferred a form of legal license for the resulting large-scale evasions of the spirit and intent of the bill (to give primacy to French in Quebec).

It is clear that the Bourassa government would have had to amend these sections of Bill 22, and to opt more clearly for one or other of the education policies inherent in chapter v (articles 40 to 44) of the bill. The Lévesque government had now, according to the White Paper, decided to establish English maternal language as the only legal basis for admission to the publicly-financed English-language schools in Quebec.

Bill 101 (Charter of the French Language),[15] was introduced in the *Assemblée nationale* on 27 April 1977, and after certain government amendments it was adopted and formally assented to on 26 August 1977. There had been criticisms advanced against Bill 22 by English-speaking groups in particular, and directed towards its use of broad administrative-law standards. The new law is more clear, precise, and categorical in its language stipulations. Bill 101, like Bill 22, opens with the declaration in article 1 that 'French is the official language of Quebec.' But where Bill 22 immediately went into general administrative provisions as to the law, Bill 101 continues with a series of categorical imperatives, about whose meaning and application there is little room for doubt or argument.

Thus, chapter II of Bill 101, Fundamental Language Rights:

Workers have a right to carry on their activities in French (Article 4)
Consumers of goods and services have a right to be informed and served in French (Article 5)
Every person eligible for instruction in Quebec has a right to receive that instruction in French (Article 6)

Again, chapter III, The Language of the Legislature and the Courts:

French is the language of the legislature and the courts in Quebec (Article 7)
Legislative bills shall be drafted in the official language. They shall also be tabled in the National Assembly, passed and assented to in that language (Article 8)
Only the French text of the statutes and regulations is official (Article 9)
An English version of every legislative bill, statute, and regulation shall be printed and published by the civil administration (Article 10)
Procedural documents issued by bodies discharging judicial or quasi-judicial functions or drawn up and sent by the advocates practising before them shall be drawn up in the official language. Such documents may, however, be drawn up in another language if the natural person for whose intention they are issued expressly consents thereto (Article 12)
The judgments rendered in Quebec by the courts and by bodies discharging judicial or quasi-judicial functions must be drawn up in French or be accompanied with a duly authenticated French version. Only the French version of the judgment is official (Article 13)

In chapter III, articles 7 to 13, the Lévesque government did what the Bourassa government manifestly did not seek to do in Bill 22. The Gendron Commission had implicitly counselled against repeal of section 133 of the BNA Act, which authorizes the use of English and French, equally, in the Quebec National Assembly and in Quebec courts. The constitutional experts consulted by the commission concluded that any such repeal applying to Quebec would be within the full legislative competence of Quebec. However the commission concluded (as did the Bourassa government in its drafting of Bill 22),[16] that, in legislation so important, it would not make sense to throw down the gauntlet to the federal government on a secondary issue that could always be dealt with later in a special law.

The language of work areas of Bill 101 include chapter IV (language of the civil administration); chapter V (language of the semi-public agencies); chapter VI (language of labour relations); chapter VII (language of commerce and business). The provisions generally follow Bill 22 but are more precise and unequivocal, thus limiting the possibilities of administrative discretion and of moderating the overriding French language requirement in the application of the measures.

Chapter VIII (language of instruction) of Bill 101 also resolves the inherent ambiguity of chapter V (language of instruction) of Bill 22, but at the expense, perhaps, of confining and limiting the element of pragmatism in administrative application that was always possible under Bill 22 precisely because of that ambiguity. Article 72 of Bill 101 establishes the basic principle that 'instruction in the kindergarten classes and in the elementary and secondary schools shall be in French.' It applies this rule to 'school bodies within the meaning of the Schedule and also ... subsidised instruction provided by institutions declared to be of public interest or recognised for purposes of grants in virtue of the Private Education Act.'

The only exceptions permitted to the basic principle of instruction in French are established by article 73. These are: a child whose father or mother received his or her elementary instruction in English in Quebec; a child whose father or mother, domiciled in Quebec on the date of the coming into force of the act, received his or her elementary instruction in English outside Quebec; a child who, before the coming into force of the act, was already 'lawfully receiving his instruction in English,' in Quebec, and the younger brothers and sisters of such a child.

Articles 72 and 73 were clearly designed to control the large-scale transfers to the English-language public schools in Quebec by the children of non-anglophone immigrants to Quebec. This had evaded the spirit and purpose of Bill 22 in its operation up to the time of enactment of Bill 101. Did these provisions of the new bill, in seeking to correct a conceived abuse permitted by the looser Bill 22, go much further than was necessary? It reached, for example, the children of English-speaking parents from the other provinces transferring to Quebec for business or other reasons. It also, for that matter, affected the children of English-speaking parents from other Commonwealth countries.

This was one of the major points of criticism levelled against Bill 101 while still in legislative committee. It was contended that these rigorous stipulations would hamper the economic growth of Quebec by creating unnecessary restraint on the free movement of businessmen and companies to Quebec from the other provinces and create gratuitous ill-will for Quebec on the part of the other provinces. It was thought that the Lévesque government might be prepared itself to amend these stipulations, voluntarily, while the measure was still in committee. But the government preferred to press on with enactment of Bill 101, reserving any softening or liberalization of these provisions to inter-provincial negotiation.

This was the genesis of the Lévesque government's plan for the so-called 'accords de réciprocité' between Quebec and the other provinces, communicated to the other provinces by letter in late July 1977, a month before the completion of the final committee stages of Bill 101. In its first form, the Lévesque plan envisaged a special disposition in the Charter of the French Language permitting the conclusion of such inter-provincial accords. These would permit access to English-language schools in Quebec for the children of anglophone parents from other provinces on condition that a similar right be accorded to the children of francophone parents from Quebec establishing themselves in those provinces.

The Lévesque proposal was immediately opposed by Prime Minister Trudeau – 'One does not negotiate on the head of children';[17] and he advised the English-speaking provinces to turn it down, and this was in fact their immediate general reaction. Premier Davis of Ontario indicated, however, that while rejecting an inter-provincial accord on language rights, he was prepared to discuss language rights with the other provincial leaders at the annual meeting of the provincial premiers at St Andrews, New Brunswick in August 1977.[18] While still rejecting Premier Lévesque's proposal for inter-provincial reciprocal accords on language of education, the premiers at St Andrews committed themselves to the principle of making arrangements for offering teaching in the minority language within their provinces and of charging their Education Ministers with the responsibility for studying what could be done to give effect to that.

At the next provincial premiers meeting, in Montreal in February 1978, the premiers passed over Prime Minister Trudeau's proposal that language rights, as such, should be entrenched in the federal constitution.[19] They accepted instead Premier Lévesque's idea that each province should be able to develop its own linguistic policy in relation to its own citizens. As *Le Devoir* commented, the premiers at their Montreal meeting recognized implicitly the language of instruction chapter of Bill 101. As the Premiers' final communiqué declared, every child of the French-speaking or the English-speaking minority in every province should have the right to receive instruction in his own language in the primary or secondary schools, wherever the number of students justified this. It also affirmed that, by reason of the exclusive competence of the provinces in education and the vast cultural and demographic differences, it was a matter for each province to define how it intended to apply that principle.

If this is not Premier Lévesque's proposal of July 1977, the substance of the original proposal is nevertheless achieved, though on an informal, intergovernmental consensus basis. Presumably for Quebec provincial law it constitutes an informal gloss on the language of chapter VIII (the language of instruction) of Bill 101, directing and controlling its application to the children of English-speaking parents from other provinces coming to reside in Quebec.

The positive-law base for this expanded or flexible interpretation of Bill 101 would no doubt be article 85, which authorizes the Quebec government, 'by regulation, [to] determine the conditions on which certain persons or categories of persons staying in Quebec temporarily, or their children, may be exempted from the application of this chapter.' (Article 86 had authorized the Quebec government to 'make regulations extending the scope of section 73 to include such persons as may be contemplated in any reciprocity agreement that may be concluded between the Government of Quebec and another province.' Such agreements could thus permit further exceptions to the French-language education requirement.)

Two legal challenges to Bill 101 soon emerged. The first was against chapter VIII (the language of instruction) and its administrative application in the case of the children of immigrants to Quebec whose maternal language was neither French nor English. The second contested the constitutionality of chapter III (the language of the legislature and the courts) (articles 7–13). Both were decided by Chief Judge Deschênes of the Superior Court of Montreal in the winter of 1977–8.

Campisi et al. v. *Procureur Général de la Province de Québec et al.*[20] was decided on 19 December 1977. The petitioners had come to Quebec in the 1950s and the 1960s, as immigrants from Italy, while still children, and had completed their primary education, already begun in Italy, in Quebec. The petitioners had applied to the local school boards in Quebec for admission of their children to the English-language schools in Quebec in terms of the special exception established in article 73(a) of Bill 101. This qualified the basic rule in article 72 that instruction in the kindergarten classes and in the elementary and secondary schools should be in French. Article 73(a) specified that a child 'whose father or mother received his or her elementary instruction in English, in Quebec' might receive his education in English if his father and mother so requested. The applications by the petitioners to their local school boards had been refused, on the school boards' interpretation of the meaning and application of chapter VIII of Bill 101.

The decision of Judge Deschênes, once again, as in the *Protestant School Board* case in 1976,[21] is a model statutory interpretation of the legislative intent and purpose of Bill 101. The Judge noted that the policy of Bill 101, as enunciated by the legislator, was clear. French is the official language, every person has the right to receive instruction in this language, and it is in this language that instruction is to be given. The exception constituted in article 73(a) must, as a disposition derogating from the basic principle of the law, receive a restrictive interpretation like any other legislation creating an exception. The provision in article 73(a) permitting instruction in English must thus be interpreted strictly, and rigorously limited to the case that it envisaged. If it were susceptible to two interpretations, that which favoured instruction in French must prevail. Looking to the facts of the case the Judge found that the petitioners, who had come from Italy during their childhood and then pursued in Quebec what remained of their primary schooling, had not 'received [their] elementary instruction in English, in Quebec' for purposes of satisfying the exception established under article 73(a) of Bill 101 of 1977.

Blaikie et al. v. *Procureur Général de la Province de Québec*,[22] was decided on 23 January 1978. The applicants were three Montreal lawyers who sought a declaration that articles 7 to 13 of Bill 101 (chapter III, the language of the legislature and the courts) were constitutionally *ultra vires* because of their conflict with article 133 of the BNA Act of 1867.

It will be remembered that the Gendron Commission had received expert legal opinion that the province could legally amend or repeal article 133 of the BNA Act so far as it purported to apply to Quebec. Provincial legislative power, under section 92(1) of the BNA Act, existed over 'the amendment from time to time, notwithstanding anything in this Act [the BNA Act], of the Constitution of the Province, except as regards the Office of Lieutenant-Governor.' The Gendron Commission had nevertheless suggested that the province should not try to derogate from the provisions of section 133 of the BNA Act in proceeding with its establishment of French as the official language of Quebec. This advice was followed by the Bourassa government with its Bill 22 which did not have anything to say directly on the language of the legislature or the courts in Quebec. The issue of Section 133 was touched, if at all, only indirectly, by way of general provisions like article 1 which provided that 'French is the official language of the Province of Quebec'; and article 2 which provided that 'where any discrepancy cannot be satisfactorily resolved by the ordinary rules of interpretation, the French text of the statutes of Quebec prevails over the English text.'

In contrast, Bill 101 goes beyond the declaration in article 1 that 'French is the official language of Quebec,' and in article 7 declares French 'the language of the legislature and the courts in Quebec.' It also stipulates that legislative bills must be drafted in the official language (French), and 'tabled in the National Assembly, passed and assented to in that language' (article 8); and that 'only the French text of the statutes and regulations is official' (article 9). Beyond that, the judgments rendered by Quebec courts must be 'drawn up in French or be accompanied with a duly authenticated French version,' while 'only the French version of the judgment is official' (article 13).

Judge Deschênes applied the classical Anglo-Saxon statutory construction that he had used in his *Protestant School Board* judgment of 1976 and in his *Campisi* judgment of 1977. The preliminary, procedural, adjectival law point was whether the applicants had a constitutional 'interest' or constitutional standing to sue sufficient to allow them to raise and to receive judgment upon the compatibility of chapter III of Bill 101 with section 133 of the BNA Act. This was resolved, elliptically, at the outset when the *Procureur Général* of Quebec withdrew his legal objection on this particular point and the judge ruled in consequence, without argument, that the applicants had *locus standi* to raise the constitutional issue. After that, there was no difficulty in concluding that chapter III of Bill 101 violated section 133 of the BNA Act – this from comparison of the texts of the articles in question (articles 7 to 13) of Bill 101 with the text of section 133 of the BNA Act.

The more substantial constitutional question remained as to whether, in the case of any inconsistency, chapter III of Bill 101 automatically amended section 133. Or, in other words, as Judge Deschênes put it, could the *Assemblée nationale* of Quebec unilaterally amend section 133 of the BNA Act? Could it, if need be, do it simply by way of later, inconsistent legislation? The Judge here took note both of the power of the federal government to legislate to amend 'the Constitution of Canada' in respect to matters within federal competence, under the BNA Act (No. 2) of 1949; and also of the power of the Quebec legislature to legislate to amend 'the Constitution of the Province' except as to the office of Lieutenant-Governor, under section 92(1) of the BNA Act.

The problem in the present case, in the Judge's view, was whether section 133 of the BNA Act constituted part of 'the Constitution of the Province.' Drawing upon the pre-Confederation history of section 133, the Judge concluded that the intention of the founding fathers of Confederation was to make it 'untouchable' within the new constitution of 1867. Judge Deschênes here referred to several cases from other Commonwealth countries

(Australia and South Africa) on the 'entrenching' of certain constitutional provisions so they could not be amended or abrogated except by some extraordinary process or extraordinary Parliamentary majority. However, the notion of constitutional 'entrenchment,' as such, was not present in British constitutional law in 1867, and does not enter into general Commonwealth constitutional law until well into the twentieth century.

The Judge also referred to the opinion of the federal government and of the nine English-speaking provinces at the federal-provincial constitutional conferences of 1950 that, in any future self-operating constitutional amending machinery for Canada, section 133 of the BNA Act should require the unanimous consent of the federal government and all the provinces for amendment. He concluded that this confirmed the understanding of the intentions of the political leaders of 1867, and he found similar support in the views of the premiers at the time of the drafting of the Victoria Charter of 1971.

An argument based on the historical intentions of the founding fathers would only be relevant and admissible, according to the classical rules of construction, if the language used in the constitutional text itself – the BNA Act – were unclear and ambiguous. To resolve this point Judge Deschênes made a brilliant survey of the writers who had looked at the power of the Quebec legislature to amend section 133 so far as it applied to Quebec. He concluded, this time perhaps more in the tradition of a civil-law jurist, that on the authority of the *doctrines* the Quebec legislature had no such power.

The notion of the divisibility of section 133 would have one part federal and subject to a unilateral federal amending power under the BNA Act (No. 2) of 1949, and one part provincial and subject to a unilateral provincial amending power under Section 92(1). The Judge rejected that notion and concluded that the two parts of the section formed two sides of the same coin and were thus constitutionally unseverable and protected from any legislative intervention, whether federal or provincial. The Judge concluded with the admonition that if indeed circumstances had changed and spirits had evolved and people did not accept being regulated any longer by the texts of 1867, such convictions should be transferred to the political processes. In the meantime, the court must read, interpret, and apply the actual constitution.

Chief Judge Deschênes' judgment in the *Blaikie* case was confirmed on appeal, by a special seven-member bench of the *Cour d'appel du Québec*, in a unanimous holding handed down on 27 November 1978.

In spite of the blow administered to an important part of Bill 101 by Judge Deschênes in the *Blaikie* case, Bill 101 still seems only a slight extension to

Bill 22. Some of the changes, particularly in language of instruction, the Bourassa government itself might have wanted to consider in any review of the first few years of application of the bill.

The language, styling, and the overall philosophy of Bill 101 are rather more direct and unequivocal, and certainly less conciliatory and tactful (relying much less on friendly persuasion).[23] That the conscious indirection of the Bourassa government had its political advantages was demonstrated clearly enough in the conflict over chapter III (the language of the legislature and the courts) of Bill 101. For Bill 22, following the recommendation of the Gendron Commission, stuck to the central issue of getting the government's French-language policy implemented and avoided the political distraction of a direct challenge to section 133 of the BNA Act. It would, in retrospect, have been wiser for the Lévesque government to have followed the Bourassa government's lead here and avoided any challenge to section 133 of the BNA Act. If it were to be a high political priority for Quebec, special legislation, separate and distinct from the government's main language policy legislation, would have been more appropriate. Faced with the initiative of the private applicants in the *Blaikie* case, the federal Attorney-General finally intervened in their favour.[24]

On the whole, however, the noticeable feature of Ottawa-Quebec relations on the language issue has been Ottawa's conscious refraining from direct challenge to the constitutionality of the Bourassa and Lévesque bills.[25] The federal government, while able to launch a challenge against Quebec's laws in this field, could hardly expect to substitute its own legislation even if it were to be successful. Perhaps the federal government realized that a fundamental political and social revolution had been achieved in Quebec by the two language laws and that Quebec is becoming as 'French' in its own way as the other provinces are now 'English.'

7

English Canada Responds

The provincial response to the Quiet Revolution is at best a delayed one, and it is selective in scope. It is a reaction in the sense that the intellectual and political initiatives for constitutional change from 1960 to November 1976 all came from Quebec. The premiers of the English-speaking provinces – Ontario excepted – have been passive bystanders to a nationalist awakening that they have never fully understood. They cannot as yet appreciate its constitutional implications.

The most significant cause of English Canada's lack of awareness was surely the continuing dominance, in Canada's English-language universities, and among the future political leaders and civil servants whom they educated, of those Keynesian ideas which tended to favour the centralization of decision-making in economic and social matters in Ottawa. Another contributing factor was the absence of any significant provincial policy research and analysis on problems of federal-provincial relations. This neglect was brought about by the absence of specialized ministries of inter-governmental affairs and of federal-provincial secretariats in most of the provincial capitals.

Ontario was the first of the English-speaking provinces to develop in a systematic and comprehensive way expertise on all aspects of federal-provincial relations. Working on constitutional, legal, cultural, linguistic, social, and economic areas, this Ontario initiative commenced in the early and mid-1960s. It paralleled the development of the provincial civil service reforms in Quebec City under the impetus of the Quiet Revolution, which meant in Quebec both the institution of a professional career civil service free from patronage and the formation of an élite bureaucratic cadre on Ottawa-Quebec relations.

Premier Robarts placed his emphasis in governmental reform not merely upon regular career civil service, but on development of para-governmental advisory and consultative groups. The Ontario Advisory Committee on Confederation was the best-known example. Established in February 1965, and lasting until Premier Robarts' retirement in 1971, it was a non-partisan, professional, and lay group chosen to advise the premier, confidentially, on federalism and specific problems of federal-provincial relations. None of its original eighteen members was clearly identifiable in party political terms. For the most part they had academic backgrounds in law, economics, or the humanities and social sciences generally. They included Professor Bora Laskin (later Chief Justice of the Supreme Court of Canada) and Dr (later Senator) Eugene Forsey. Premier Robarts seemed to use the committee both for the development of alternative policy constructs and as a testing-ground for his own ideas on future Ontario policies on Confederation.

The committee's confidentiality was a result, it is understood, of advice from Jean Lesage. Lesage had apparently had reason to regret non-civil-service academic advisers' communicating directly with the press on matters of policy. Nevertheless, the Ontario Advisory Committee on Confederation did publish two volumes of background papers and reports – *The Confederation Challenge* – in 1967 and 1970,[1] covering the full range of federal-provincial relations.

Something of the dialectical character of the committee's internal discussions and the development of its own reasoned recommendations to the Premier is indicated in those volumes. There will often be at least two distinct approaches to the one problem – the more orthodox view, and an approach which incorporates some of the thrust of Quebec proposals – without any necessary attempt to decide between those different views. This is noticeable in such issues as the nature, organization, and composition of the Supreme Court of Canada; the rôle of the provinces in extra-provincial or trans-national cultural and commercial accords or contracts, and its impact on the foreign affairs power in a federal system; and the obligations and competences of the federal government and the provinces in civil liberties.

These matters were becoming points of conflict between the federal government and Quebec by the late 1960s. The wide-ranging advice of the committee established a basis for the Ontario government's understanding of Quebec's claims, without any obligation to accept those claims, creating a particularly harmonious Ontario-Quebec relationship that persisted into the 1970s, at a time of great strain in Ottawa-Quebec relations.

In terms of governmental action in Ontario, not much emerged from the Robarts era in regard to Confederation. It was not a period when the federal government was disposed to move in constitutional matters, except with the Victoria Charter of 1971. Its proposals were considered by Quebec to be both 'too little, too late' and an unacceptable 'strait-jacket' for the future.

William Davis, who succeeded John Robarts as Premier in 1971, did not seem especially concerned with constitutional law during his first years in office. After the election of the *Parti québécois* in Quebec in November 1976 – and perhaps because as leader of a minority government, Davis could expect defeat in the legislature and a provincial election during 1977 – the Premier seemed to desire the mantle of a contemporary 'father of Confederation' so successfully worn by Robarts. He followed Robarts by forming an Ontario Advisory Committee on Confederation to work out specific proposals for the Ontario government's approach to federal-provincial relations and the BNA Act generally. He also financed the organization of a public conference 'Destiny Canada,' with the same general objective.

The Advisory Committee, formed early in 1977, was a predominantly political or 'lay' group, unlike his predecessor's non-partisan 'expert' committee. The Davis committee did not stop with identification of the main policy alternatives, the quantification of their relative social cost, and the assessment of their operational utility, but entered directly into the Confederation debate by advancing its own program.

The difference in style and experience of the two committees is amply reflected in their personnel. The chairman, Ian Macdonald – then a senior provincial civil servant and now president of York University, Toronto, and the executive secretary, Don Stevenson, a provincial civil servant, were the same. However, there were only two professors among the thirteen other members of the Davis Committee. Only one other person, former Governor-General Roland Michener (who had earlier been Speaker of the House of Commons), had any claims to constitutional expertise. Perhaps the relative lack of technical expertise helps explain the relative freedom from self-doubt or equivocation in the committee's first proposals, officially presented in April 1978.

The committee suggested two broad options for Canadian Confederation: 'either a wholesale decentralization of power in favour of regional and provincial autonomy, or fundamental reform of federal institutions to make them more responsive to regional concerns and interests in the evolution of national policy.'

In its first report, the committee selected the second alternative advanced – 'fundamental reform of federal institutions' – through, in the committee's own words, 'constitutionally involving the provincial governments in the formulation of, and responsibility for, national policy decisions, as well as in the organization of vital national institutions such as the Supreme Court and the major regulatory agencies.'

The key was to be replacement of the Senate by a new 'House of Provinces' which 'would have real authority derived from the elected governments of the provinces.' Its members were to 'be appointed by and represent the provincial governments.' Why an appointive federal upper house rather than an elective one, appointive legislative bodies generally being considered anachronistic today? The committee only says, elliptically, that 'the option of an elected second chamber was considered and rejected by the Committee on the grounds that it would create more problems than it would solve, making the existing system more complex and competing with the House of Commons and the provincial governments.'

The new 'House of Provinces' was to have thirty members. Six would be appointed by the Ontario government and six by the Quebec government; with provincial premiers and cabinet ministers having the right to sit in the new house, presumably concurrently with their seats in the provincial legislatures. The 'House of Provinces' was to have a right of suspensive veto for up to one year over all bills passed by the House of Commons, but no power to initiate legislation. It was to have the power to confirm or reject all federal appointments to the Supreme Court of Canada and to federal regulatory bodies including the National Energy Board, the Canadian Transport Commission, the Canadian Radio-Television and Telecommunications Commission, and the Bank of Canada.

The plan, of course, did nothing at all to meet Quebec claims of the 1960s for a key rôle in federal institutions such as the Senate. Six Quebec seats out of thirty in the new 'House of Provinces' is hardly an adequate response on that point. The plan also compromised its own claims to being a reform of existing federal institutions by retaining the existing, much-criticized 'patronage' appointments to the Senate. Appointment to a legislative chamber is no substitute for direct popular election. One wonders if provincial patronage in appointments to the 'House of Provinces' would be any more commendable than the federal government's record on appointments to the Senate.

The plan also had something to say on the Supreme Court of Canada: 'The Committee discussed the possibility of the establishment of a separate constitutional court, but rejected it on the grounds that the power of the House of Provinces to approve nominations to the Supreme Court of Canada would make the court a more truly national institution.'

Now one may well agree with the case against the suitability for Canada of the special constitutional court which has worked so well in post-war Europe.

However, the committee's explanation neither reveals its reasoning nor supports the point being made. Perhaps it simply reflects the non-technical character of the committee and its members. The committee went on, in any case, to affirm its belief that 'the court system should reflect the division of jurisdiction inherent in a federal state. It, therefore, recommends that provincial governments make appointments to all courts other than the Supreme Court [of Canada] and the Federal Court.'

The committee had certain thoughts on the need for an entrenched bill of rights and for a new constitutional amending procedure. These proposals contained little that was new, except perhaps for the recommendation on 'language rights,' that 'each child of the French-speaking or English-speaking minority should be entitled, whenever numbers warrant, to an education in his or her language in the primary and the secondary schools in any province.'[2]

In fact, at the First Ministers' constitutional conference, in Ottawa from 30 October to 1 November 1978, Premier Davis showed himself in no way beholden to sponsor or even to repeat the recommendations of his committee. Such non-elected committees are evidently in his view (and correctly so, it may be argued) there to put forward alternative policy constructs. They can never be a substitute for the government's own constitutional obligations in decision-making and ultimate policy choice. Thus, not a word was heard from Premier Davis on the proposed new 'House of Provinces,' to 'be appointed by and represent the provincial governments.' Nothing seems to die so quickly as constitutional ideas that have passed their time. Premier Bennett was left in splendid isolation invoking the case for Senate 'reform,' while Davis joined with the remaining premiers in rallying to Trudeau's consigning of the Senate 'to a low back-burner.' Attention could be focussed, at the February 1979 constitutional conference, on substantive questions of division of legislative powers between the federal government and the provinces.

The official views of the Progressive Conservative party of Canada are close to the proposals in the Davis plan. This similarly suggests not merely close liaison between the two groups concerned, but also common authorship or at least common sources. (Flora MacDonald, the chairman of the PC caucus committee on federal-provincial relations, represents an Ontario constituency in the House of Commons.) The Conservative party paper, *The Constitution and National Unity*, appeared in early 1978.[3] It opens with a statement of the 'need to accommodate regional diversity in Canada through two significant changes': 'direct provincial participation in certain national institutions and agencies, principally by reform of the Senate into a House of the Provinces,' and 'formal recognition that a federal system requires regular public consultation among responsible governments, through federal-provincial conferences.'

It declares, somewhat rhetorically, that 'the legitimacy of the existing constitution has been substantially eroded,' and that 'Canadians in many regions have felt unrepresented in federal councils.' The main prescription for the alleged constitutional malaise – a 'House of the Provinces' – seems taken directly from the Davis plan, though it is not as extreme or categorical on the composition of that new body. The paper modestly limits itself to the demand that the 'majority' of members of the House be 'delegated by the provincial government,' and concedes that the federal government might also be permitted to appoint 'a small number of delegates.' Like the Davis plan, the paper also disposes very quickly (and elliptically) of the case for direct, popular election to this new upper house. If the house were directly and popularly elected it 'would be very difficult' for the lower house to 'hold the Federal Cabinet fully accountable to it and to the people.' Why would that be so? The paper makes the assertion without any supporting demonstration and then goes immediately to its next argument against direct, popular elections.

If elections to the new upper house were to be held at the same time as a federal election, 'the party composition of the second chamber would closely reflect that of the Commons.' But the paper does not consider the idea of staggering the terms of office, and hence the timing of the particular general election at which the members of the new house would be elected. This is an arrangement common with elections to federal upper houses elsewhere.

The paper also rejects out-of-hand the alternative possibility of direct, popular elections to the new house synchronized with provincial general elections: 'those elected would have no mandate to speak for their provincial governments.' But would that matter? Those elected in this way to the new house would have a far greater degree of legitimation conferred by direct election. Their mandate to speak for the people of their province on federal matters would thus exceed that of the provincial governments. Is that the problem? Do provincial governments, rather than the elected members of Parliament, have the best claim to 'represent' the people of the province in federal institutions? If the committee thinks so, this should be stated, rather than letting this notion operate as an unstated assumption.

The paper goes on to claim that the 'basic legitimacy' of the Supreme Court of Canada has been 'eroded' by the 'unilateral appointment of Justices of the Supreme Court of Canada by the Federal Government.' A remedy for the future might be an 'obligation' on the part of the federal government to 'consult with the government of any province from which an appointment is proposed,' and also a right of the proposed new House of the Provinces to veto any such appointments. This veto right is also advanced for federal government appointments to the executive boards of key agencies. All these proposals are advanced in the interest of a 'revitalized confederation.'

The paper seems to down-grade the importance of constitutional revision in federal-provincial divisions of legislative competence – sections 91 and 92 of the BNA Act. It notes the 'almost complete break-down in the "watertight compartments" view of federalism'; 'responsibility for a great many important policy functions is now shared.' There is a 'resulting need for joint decision-making and coordination.' If so, this emphasis differs from other approaches to constitutional change. It suggests that the distinction between federal institutional changes and changes in law-making competences of the different levels of government is not essentially one of tactical priorities (as, seemingly, with the Davis plan). Rather there is a recognition that the postulation of foolproof, *a priori* lists of law-making competences of the different governments is merely a verbal exercise, given the realities of contemporary 'mixed' governmental decision-making.

A distinctive British Columbia position on the BNA Act and on change in the federal constitution emerged after the election of the Social Credit government in November 1975. It was initially linked to then still-continuing federal-provincial discussions on 'patriation' of the BNA Act and development of a new amending formula. In a paper, *What is British Columbia's position on the Constitution of Canada?*, issued in November 1976,[4] Premier Bennett developed his 'five region' concept of the Canadian federal system. This meant 'the approval of each of Ontario, Quebec, two of the three Prairie Provinces, two of the four Atlantic Provinces, and British Columbia for constitutional amendments.' The paper noted inadequate recognition of 'the emergence of the West' in the Victoria Charter proposals.

Other implications of the 'five region' concept were correction of a 'manifestly unfair imbalance' in the Senate by an increase in the number of BC senators from six to twelve, and making the Senate a 'more viable part of the federal law-making process.' Though this latter suggestion was not spelled out, there was laudatory reference to the West German federal upper house, the *Bundesrat*. It was described as being 'directly representative of the state governments and [having] extensive powers of veto over all matters affecting state interests as well as a suspensive power over national matters.' Premier Bennett then turned to the Supreme Court of Canada and proposed its increase from nine to ten judges so that 'at all times at least one of the Judges be appointed from the Bar or the Bench of the Province of British Columbia, two Judges appointed from among the three Prairie Provinces, three from Ontario, three from Quebec, and one from the Atlantic Provinces.'

The Premier also criticized various federal Crown corporations and federal administrative agencies – the CBC, the CRTC, the Canadian Development Corporation, and the Bank of Canada. He saw them as 'little more than national government institutions rather than being genuinely federal in nature,' and demanded that their governing bodies be appointed 'by a process involving Provincial Governments as well as the Government of Canada.' He also asked for 'strengthening of jurisdiction of Provincial Governments in the taxation of primary production from lands, mines, minerals, and forests,' and for 'a greater degree of provincial involvement in immigration.'

Bennett submitted a brief to the Pépin-Roberts Commission at its Vancouver hearings in February 1978. He had consolidated and extended his 'five region' proposal in a general bid for the 'restructuring and development of genuine Federal-Provincial institutions,' and for the 'revision and modernization of our Constitution.' This time, there were laudatory references not only to the West German but also to the Swiss federal system. The Canadian Senate should be 'restructured to become a "provincial house,"' with an absolute veto over 'amendments to the Constitution, and laws that require a national consensus or laws that directly affect the provinces,' a suspensive veto over all other laws, and a 'function' regarding appointments to the Supreme Court and federal boards and commissions. The Supreme Court is to be increased to ten judges with at all times a judge appointed from BC. While the Premier had not, as yet, a categorical proposal regarding the constitution of the new Senate, he indicated a house 'directly representative of the provincial governments,' or one with its 'membership ... appointed by the provinces, or ... popularly elected.'[5]

By May 1978 Bennett's constitutional thinking had evolved even further. In an address to the Men's Canadian Club of Vancouver on 17 May he rejected both 'Quebec separation with "sovereignty-association"' and 'the federal government's so-called "*status-quo* federalism."' He offered instead what he called 'consultative federalism – the third option for Canada.' The term 'consultative federalism' is rather vague, and it is necessary to dig into Bennett's speech to try to give it some more or less precise connotation. Once again there was genuflection towards West Germany and Switzerland in the name of a constitutional restructuring 'to give the Provinces an effective voice in the decision-making process in Ottawa,' and in order that 'national policy-making should not be the private preserve of the federal government.'

And then it all tumbled out again: the Senate is to become a 'provincial house ... truly a provincial body,' in order to have 'legitimacy, viewed from both the federal and Provincial Governments' perspective.' Its representation should be based on a 'system which would give to each of the five regions of Canada an equal number of Senate seats.' In this way, the Senate would 'have the full confidence of Provincial Governments as their voice in the federal law-making process.' There is a defensive explanation that the 'five region' Confederation would not necessarily mean the abolition of five of the existing provinces or even regional government *per se* or 'some new tier of government.' Each of Premier Bennett's five regions would merely have 'its own representation' in the Senate, on the Supreme Court, and on federal boards and commissions. Bennett does make an opening to Quebec by indicating that the division of federal and provincial legislative competences must be 'flexible enough to allow the Government of Quebec to legislate on matters of language and culture within that Province.' However, this does not mean that he is 'proposing "special status" for Quebec.'

Clearly his constitutional thinking was no longer a somewhat simplistic claim for more BC representatives in the Senate and on the Supreme Court and other federal bodies. He now makes a more general demand for decentralization of the federal system and for inclusion of the provincial governments in the federal government's decision-making processes. He passes over the interesting issues of constitutional theory necessarily involved in such a demand. Doesn't the federal House of Commons have an electoral mandate from BC voters quite as much as from voters in the other nine provinces? Cannot the federal government lay claim, legitimately, to speak for BC voters on federal constitutional matters quite as much, if not more, than the BC provincial government?

The essence of a federal system is that it assigns different constitutional rôles and missions to different levels of government. There is a national governmental mandate that necessarily covers BC on national matters; whereas the provincial government mandate is limited, and properly so, to provincial matters.

Some aspects of Bennett's proposals seem redolent of an old-fashioned 'compact' theory of Canadian Confederation. In this case, however, it is not a French-English compact, for which there might be some colour of historical validity; but a ten-province compact which would be without historical justification. Such ideas echo the constitutional theory of the fifteenth and sixteenth centuries, before the evolution of federalism and democratic thought on plural-constitutional associations. The analogue is the Holy Roman Empire where a collection of perpetually feuding local leaders swore fealty – but usually failed to render allegiance and obedience – to a nominal emperor. In his brief to the 1978 First Ministers' constitutional conference, Premier Bennett's constitutional demands take on a sharper, more particularistic note. The BC brief – nine little booklets with variegated, brightly-hued covers – has the appearance of a series of public relations releases or consumer reports rather than of a conventional legal document. The first booklet, 'Towards a revised constitution for Canada,' sets the tone for the whole. It declares that 'western alienation and maritime regional disparities are not merely catch phrases,' and that the 'difficulties within our federal system will not be resolved through minor tinkering so as to give a few more Senate seats here and there or by moving a few federal public servants out of Ottawa into the provinces in the name of decentralisation.' It concludes by solemnly warning against what it identifies as 'constitutional "overstuffing."' Bennett is opposed to entrenching 'basic human rights, including language rights' in the constitution!

Everything else in the 'brief' is eminently predictable: we have a *reprise* of his 'five region' conception of a new Canadian Confederation, with British Columbia as one of those five regions; the Supreme Court of Canada is to be increased from nine to eleven judges, with 'membership ... based primarily on merit but ... drawn from all the five regions of Canada'; and the existing Senate is to be transformed into a *Bundesrat*. Its members are to become the creatures of the provincial governments – wholly appointed by provincial governments and removable on the same basis – and with BC naming one-fifth of the total membership. This public embracing of an aspect of German constitutionalism is justified on the basis of 'the personal observation and study of the West German system undertaken by some members of the British Columbia Government.' This apparently refers to a visit to West Germany and Switzerland, for 'all but one day of two weeks' – made by the provincial Minister of Consumer Affairs.

This is not a very serious way in which to conduct research in comparative constitutional law or to attempt to reach valid conclusions for Canada from foreign experience. It is evident also from the reaction, or lack of reaction, by other premiers, that his approach may be hardly calculated to win friends and influence people in the hard bargaining of a First Ministers' conference! The premiers of the three prairie provinces and the four Atlantic provinces were somewhat less than enthusiastic about the prospect of being lumped together into regions. They would thereby be reduced, in one blow, from their present constitutional parity with Ontario and Quebec to mere segments of a region. They would have only a fraction of the constitutional status of Ontario, Quebec, and – lest we forget – British Columbia.

Prime Minister Trudeau also gave short shrift to Bennett's Senate 'reform' plan in the short list of subjects to be discussed at the resumed constitutional conference in February 1979. As Trudeau remarked: 'The ministers are wise, they won't spend too much time on [the Senate] because it didn't look as though a consensus was going to develop ... I'm advising them to put it aside so that at the February conference we will have reports on things on which they can make progress.'

At their annual meeting in April 1976 the premiers of the four western provinces set up a joint Task Force on Constitutional Trends. It was designed to 'prepare a detailed inventory of ... apparent intrusions' of the federal government, involving the 'increasing tendency, perceived at that time, of the Government of Canada initiating federal legislation in subject areas which historically and constitutionally have been considered to be within the Provincial sphere.' The annual reports that have emerged from this task force are the products of civil servants rather than of political leaders, and have a high degree of sophistication. They are essentially case- or problem-oriented and empirically based, and avoid political rhetoric, even if the categorization of federal 'intrusions' necessarily involves political judgment.

The first report ranges over consumer and corporate affairs; resources; housing, urban affairs, and land use; economic development; communications; demography and immigration, manpower and training, and labour; and the administration of justice.

Thus, on communications, it is indicated that the western governments agree that 'cable television services which do not directly involve the relay, retransmission, or amplification of broadcast signals should be subject to provincial control. So should educational communications which are carried out by means of cable or wire technology.'

On immigration, it is proposed that 'demographic and immigration policies must be coordinated with regional economic development, housing programmes, transportation programmes, and urban development and land policies,' and that the provinces 'have an interest in controlling ... numbers of immigrants, and immigrant employment qualifications.'[6]

There is a section of the report headed 'Interventions by the Government of Canada before the Supreme Court of Canada in opposition to Provincial Legislation.' This lists ten cases from 1973 to 1977, including *Canadian Industrial Gas and Oil Ltd.* v. *Saskatchewan*[7] where Ottawa attempted unsuccessfully to be joined as a plaintiff-appellant instead of just as intervenant;

and *Central Canada Potash Co. Ltd.* v. *Saskatchewan*[8] (where Ottawa took the unprecedented step of becoming a plaintiff in the action, calling witnesses and adducing evidence at the trial, thus influencing the set of facts on which the case was founded). The report quotes Premier Blakeney of Saskatchewan's statement to the First Ministers' meeting of 13 and 14 December 1976 that the federal position in these resource cases demonstrated a 'systematic and deliberate attempt to destroy, through court action, the provincial rights of resource ownership.'[9] (See pages 102–5.)

In its second report in April 1978, the task force adverted not merely to the 'intrusions' set out in the first report, but also established a new, detailed list that included subjects like fisheries and also some advice on 'Mechanisms ... to prevent or lessen such intrusions in the future.' These mechanisms included the proposal that the federal government's Federal-Provincial Relations Office should examine all federal policy and program proposals 'in their early stages of development.' The Office should ask the following questions: '(1) is the proposed policy or programme constitutional? (2) will it duplicate, overlap, or conflict with provincial programmes already in place? (3) what will be required to ensure adequate consultation with the provinces?'

This time, the criticisms of federal goverment interventions are sharpened: 'The provinces are concerned over the recent practice by which the Federal Government has actually aligned itself as a plaintiff with parties in court cases challenging the constitutionality of provincial resource legislation. It is felt that the co-plaintiff strategy represents an unnecessarily aggressive approach by the Federal Government to this matter.'

The report cites Ottawa's intervention as a co-plaintiff in the *Central Canada Potash* case as an example of 'an aggressive federal stance toward provincial taxation and control of the provinces' natural resources that remains unreconciled.'[10]

When the western premiers go beyond the listing of complaints arising in specific situations, the problems in developing and maintaining a common western position on Canadian federalism become clear. The Canada West Foundation is a private foundation apparently financed by the four western provincial governments and by key commercial companies doing business in western Canada. It seems to act as a bridge in building a common constitutional platform for the four provincial governments involving specific proposals for change in existing federal institutions. There was to be a great public conference similar to the one financed by Premier Davis in Toronto in the spring of 1977. This western public conference, entitled 'Alternatives Canada' was held in Banff, in March 1978.[11] As with the Toronto conference, the credentials of the conference were established by having a list of specially invited delegates and observers whose expenses were generally assumed by the foundation. The main thrust of the conference came, however, from formal addresses by the provincial premiers from which a common western attitude could be drawn. There was a conference discussion paper prepared by three Alberta professors without, apparently, any direct discussion or consultation with the four provincial governments concerned. This discussion paper endorsed a 'House of Provinces,' to be composed of provincial delegations led by provincial premiers and 'casting a single weighted vote' per delegation, but also (perhaps unwisely), ran the whole gamut of constitutional change.[12]

The *coup de grâce* to the discussion paper and perhaps to the notion of a common western set of demands was administered, coolly and elegantly, by Premier Lougheed of Alberta in his address to the conference.[13]

Lougheed rejected the extreme suggestions for a wholesale scrapping of the federal constitution: 'I think that overall the British North America Act has served us pretty well.' On the issue of replacing the Senate by a new 'House of Provinces' he observed:

I just don't think it will work too well. The elected people are going to have to be responsible in the Alberta Legislature. I would like you to think about how it would work if you delegated the responsibility to a Chamber in Ottawa, independent or separated from the direct confrontation at the elected level between the two levels of government on tough negotiations ... It can't be delegated, it has to be direct confrontation and hard bargaining and negotiation.

Lougheed thus rejected any notion of an upper house nominated by provincial governments because he felt federal-provincial negotiations must be conducted from a direct power base. This meant retention of the federal-provincial premiers' conferences as the principal arena for interaction, negotiation, and eventual accommodation. There was no room for a rival 'delegated' body purporting to represent provincial interests.

Lougheed expressed reservations regarding the Supreme Court's decision in the *Canadian Industrial Gas and Oil* case, and felt the time had come to establish a provincial jurisdiction in indirect taxation. He also suggested that 'some fetters have to be put on the judgment of Chief Justice Laskin in the Supreme Court of Canada with regard to the emergency powers of the federal government'; and he concluded that 'I do concur with the idea that the Supreme Court of Canada has to be changed into a constitutional court.' He was the only provincial premier, outside Quebec, to focus upon the Supreme

Court rather than the Senate as the key federal institution for arbitration of federal-provincial power conflicts.

As for the 'region' concept of Canadian Confederation, whether a 'five region' combination or any other number: 'keep in mind it's provinces, not regions ... Consider delegated powers as a possible option, don't throw the whole BNA Act out the window, look at it in its total balance and its division of powers which are generally working.'

On specific constitutional changes: 'Restructure the Supreme Court of Canada: Provide the provinces with indirect tax and develop a direct provincial appointment to major federal agencies' (up to forty per cent representation from the provincial level on federal regulatory agencies like the Wheat Board, the National Energy Board, and the Canadian Transport Commission, he suggested). As a last key point, Lougheed didn't think 'special status' for one province alone would work; but he allowed that 'there is justifiable reason, granted in different degrees, of a certain element of special status for all provinces.'

In his brief to the 1978 First Ministers' constitutional conference[14] Lougheed restated these ideas in a more comprehensive and integrated form. He placed his emphasis on the division of legislative powers between the federal government and the provinces. He expressed the need to discuss these issues in conjunction with federal institutional questions, particularly the Supreme Court of Canada. As a realistic and pragmatic political leader Lougheed was not disposed to waste time on the trivial or inconsequential. There is not a word on 'reform' of the Senate. Instead, in his examination of existing federal institutions, he goes straight to the Supreme Court: 'it is important that the court which interprets constitutional provisions be clearly seen to reflect the federal nature of the country. It must be cognisant of not only the views of the federal government but also of the provincial governments ... The function of arbiter of constitutional issues would best be carried out through a special constitutional court which is completely separate from the Supreme Court of Canada and which is representative of all parts of the country.'

In the direction that he thus gives to constitutional change, Lougheed confirms the suspicion that current provincial dissatisfaction may be less a complaint about the constitution or division of powers, than a concern with recent Supreme Court decisions. Lougheed's language is deliberately modest and understated: 'interpretation of the constitution may have an impact upon the division of constitutional responsibilities and jurisdiction assigned to the federal and provincial governments'; but his actual prescription is, at first sight, rather startling. A new *constitutional court* is to be appointed 'from a previously agreed upon panel of experienced superior court judges ... The constitutional court panel could consist of approximately forty to fifty members ... Each provincial government would submit a list of judges to the federal government ... The federal government would then select the judges for the constitutional panel from among the list of names proposed by a provincial government.'

How would the new constitutional court function? According to the Alberta brief, 'A constitutional court consisting of seven members selected at random from amongst all members of the panel would be convened to hear questions or cases of a constitutional nature. Having heard the case, those seven members would not be eligible to hear another case until all other members have participated in a constitutional case.'

It is all very complex. If ever applied in real life, it would make nonsense of the concept of constitutional jurisprudence as an orderly system of precedents evolving through case-by-case development by a continuing tribunal of judges. The proposed new constitutional court would be one of a kind: there is nothing like it in either common-law or civil-law jurisdictions. It bears no resemblance whatsoever in organization or style to the special constitutional courts now operating so successfully in various European countries. No tribunal, except the *Cour de Cassation* (*toutes chambres réunies*), would be larger in terms of sheer numbers of members in the panel of judges to be established. It would amount, in effect, to a permanent merry-go-round. Each bench of seven judges, after rendering judgment in a case, would be replaced by another bench of seven until the whole panel of forty to fifty judges was exhausted.

And yet, in spite of these patent excesses, the Alberta proposal does focus attention on the profound dissatisfaction with the judgments on division of powers rendered by current Supreme Court majorities. This dissatisfaction is also reflected in a parallel suggestion, in section XII of the Alberta brief, that 'the protection of fundamental human rights continues to be the responsibility of Parliament and the Provincial Legislatures, rather than a bill of rights entrenched in the Constitution.'

As the explanatory comments to section XII note: 'the rôle of legislatures in protecting rights would be significantly diminished if a bill of rights were to be entrenched in the Constitution. The principle of legislative supremacy would be undermined. The courts would become the chief forum for determining what is permissible under an entrenched bill of rights. To a great extent, this has been the case in the United States. One of the consequences has been to involve the courts in the adjudication of a wide range of social questions, which in the interests of society are best debated and resolved in legislatures.'

If the proposals for the forty- to fifty-member panel had been advanced by any other province than Alberta, one might have had fears for the continuance of a workable federal system. Lougheed, however, uses research staff proposals to focus attention on particular issues. He has a keen tactical sense of knowing when in a conference to press a debating point to its logical conclusion, and when to concede gracefully because it has succeeded in its main objectives or else become untenable.

In the 1978 constitutional conference, Lougheed did not canvass the issue of institutional changes involving the court. If his main concern was to 'correct' the centralist decisions of the Supreme Court, the same result could also be achieved by a new re-definition and re-allocation of the heads of legislative power under sections 91 and 92 of the BNA Act. Prime Minister Trudeau, half-way through the conference, agreed to a joint federal-provincial working committee for report back in February 1979. It was to consider a list of seven current areas of conflict over division of powers. These coincided in substantial measure with Alberta's own short list, and it became constitutionally inelegant – almost an exercise in constitutional overkill – to press for reform of the Supreme Court.

8
Quebec et al. v. Ottawa

The extreme economic difficulties of the western post-industrial societies from the mid-1970s onwards stemmed from a combination of international and domestic factors. The emergence of the OPEC countries and their decision in 1973 to exact a marked raise in world oil prices coincided almost exactly with the prolonged Watergate crisis in the United States, the weakening of American leadership, and the accompanying decline in American investor confidence.

In Canada, Prime Minister Trudeau's belief in strong federal executive power as a counter to rapidly burgeoning French-Canadian nationalism seemed to confirm and reinforce the Keynesian thinking which had preached the concentration of economic planning and decision-making powers in the central government. Fresh clashes between the federal government and the provinces were made almost inevitable when the Trudeau government responded to the general economic crisis by introducing its controversial proposals for legislating federal controls upon wages and prices in the autumn of 1975 (an idea it had opposed in the 1974 election campaign).

A new generation of English-speaking provincial leaders, mostly from rival political parties, felt that this action extended still further Ottawa's centralizing tendencies. These had been evident during the Depression of the 1930s, the wartime planning period, and the post-war era of controls. Most of these premiers were young, dynamic, and confident. They decided to resist what they felt to be Keynesian imperatives carried to an absurd conclusion. For the first time their debating positions coincided almost exactly with those of Quebec under Robert Bourassa or even René Lévesque.

The English-speaking premiers favoured a devolution of decision-making power and the safeguarding and maintenance of provincial autonomy in economic planning. The dialectical process in the emergence of new federal constitutional law-in-action is to be seen in a number of key conflicts, beginning with the announcement of the federal wage and price control measures in October 1975. In general we can see strong exercises in federal law-making power producing equally strong provincial reactions. Quebec and the English-speaking provinces consolidated or coalesced for these purposes, with the federal Supreme Court waiting in the wings to be invoked if the federal government thought it necessary or useful.

The idea of federal wage and price controls would seem to involve sections 92(13) and 92(16) of the BNA Act 'Property and Civil Rights in the Province,' and 'matters of a merely local or private nature in the Province.' The Privy Council, in its *Board of Commerce Act* ruling of 1922, with Lord Haldane writing the opinion of the Board,[1] had held that a 1919 federal statute authorizing the establishment of price-fixing in the clothing industry was beyond the powers of the federal government. Lord Haldane, like Lord Watson before him, was always sensitive to claims of provincial rights; yet he made a point of recognizing that in a 'sufficiently great emergency' the federal government must have constitutional power to 'deal adequately with that emergency for the safety of the Dominion as a whole.' The Privy Council's reservations about the 1919 price controls stemmed principally from the fact that those controls were applied as wartime measures when the war had already ended. There was also a disinclination – understandable before the Great Depression changed thinking on the matter – to recognize that an economic crisis could be every bit as prejudicial to the national interest as a war.

When Prime Minister Trudeau announced the federal wage and price controls in October 1975, he was at the height of his political popularity and authority. His minority government (1972–4) had been re-elected in 1974 with a clear majority, and there had been fairly general public and editorial support for the control measures in the face of a seeming international and national economic recession. The provincial premiers were little inclined to undertake a direct, frontal challenge to the constitutionality of the measures. Such provincial unhappiness as existed was vented, instead, in lateral assaults upon certain aspects of the controls legislation. Nevertheless, the matter did end up before the Supreme Court of Canada.

The Ontario government had placed Ontario public servants under the wages jurisdiction of the federal Anti-Inflation Board established under the legislation. However, this action had been effected by an Ottawa-Ontario agreement made under the authority of the federal legislation. School teachers in Renfrew, Ontario challenged the legality of the agreement. They questioned the ability of the Ontario government to delegate to Ottawa law-making power over the wages of Ontario public servants – in effect, an inter-govern-mental delegation of powers. The federal Attorney-General nonetheless concluded that the constitutionality of the federal Anti-Inflation Act itself might be dragged before the courts, and he accordingly seized the legal initia-tive and himself referred the matter to the Supreme Court of Canada for a ruling on constitutionality.

In its decision handed down in July 1976,[2] the Supreme Court held, by a seven to two vote, that the federal act was constitutional. It also ruled, by a nine to nil vote (for reasons relating to delegation of law-making powers between the two levels of government that do not here concern us), that the Ottawa-Ontario agreement was invalid.

On the constitutionality of the federal Anti-Inflation Act, the Supreme Court heard arguments from a number of provincial governments as well as the federal government. While the Ontario government joined with Ottawa in defending the constitutionality of the act, two provinces in particular, Quebec and Saskatchewan, gave only qualified support to federal law-mak-ing power in the area concerned, arguing that the federal act could only be supported on the basis of being emergency legislation. British Columbia seemed to suggest in its oral argument before the court that the onus was on the federal government affirmatively to prove the existence of an emergency and that it had not proved that in the present case.

The reference here is to the so-called 'emergency' concept of the federal government's 'Peace, Order, and good Government' power under section 91 of the BNA Act. In the seven to two judgment upholding the constitution-ality of the federal act, the 'emergency' concept was a key point of division or differentiation between the majority and the minority judges and even within the ranks of the majority judges themselves. In upholding the federal act, Chief Justice Laskin wrote a majority opinion that was concurred in by three other justices (Judson, Spence, and Dickson). There was a further majority opinion, written by Justice Ritchie and concurred in by two other justices (Martland and Pigeon). Finally, Justice Beetz wrote a dissenting opinion that was concurred in by Justice de Grandpré.

Chief Justice Laskin wrote the key majority opinion which carried (includ-ing his own vote) the support of four out of the nine judges. He addressed himself to the main question raised in argument before the court: whether the general 'Peace, Order, and good Government' power of the federal gov-ernment could support the present act:[3]

In my opinion, this court would be unjustified in concluding, on the submissions in this case and on all the material put before it, that the Parliament of Canada did not have a rational basis for regarding the Anti-Inflation Act as a measure which, in its judgment, was temporarily necessary to meet a situation of economic crisis imperilling the well-being of the people of Canada as a whole and requiring Parliament's stern intervention in the interests of the country as a whole. That there may have been other periods of crisis in which no similar action was taken is beside the point.

Chief Justice Laskin here seems to echo the US doctrine of judicial self-restraint and the obligation of a court to defer to the popular will as expressed in the enactments of legislative majorites 'unless it can be said that a rational and fair man necessarily would admit that a statute proposed would infringe fundamental principles as they have been understood by the traditions of our people and our law' (Holmes's words). The thrust of Chief Justice Laskin's opinion is clear: the act is a valid expression of the federal government's general legislative power under the 'Peace, Order, and good Government' clause. The Chief Justice goes beyond that, however, to suggest that the constitutionality of the act under section 91 could be rested further upon the federal government's 'jurisdiction over monetary policy' (presumably under sub-sections 3, 4, 14, and 15), and upon the federal jurisdiction over 'the regulation of trade and commerce' (sub-section 2). He accordingly concludes:

The fact that there had been rising inflation at the time federal action was taken, that inflation is regarded as a monetary phenomenon and that monetary policy is admittedly within exclusive federal jurisdiction persuades me that the Parliament of Canada was entitled, in the circumstances then prevailing and to which I have already referred, to act as it did from the springboard of its jurisdiction over monetary policy and, I venture to add, with additional support from its power in relation to the regulation of trade and commerce.[4]

He rejected in passing an argument submitted by counsel for one of the private parties, the Ontario School Teachers. (Other private interest group parties included the Canadian Labour Congress and other labour groups.) The teachers had maintained that the federal government was constitutionally wrong in proceeding with its own federal Anti-Inflation Act without having first tried to proceed on a cooperative basis with the provinces in dealing with the problem. The Chief Justice noted in regard to the submission:

It was put in terms of an objection to the validity of the federal legislation, the proposition being that inflation was too sweeping a subject to be dealt with by a single authority, i.e., the federal Parliament, and that the proper constitutional approach, at least as a first approach, was through federal-provincial cooperation in terms of their respective powers under the respective enumerations in sections 91 and 92. If this is meant to suggest that Parliament cannot act in relation to inflation even in a crisis situation, I must disagree. No doubt, federal-provincial cooperation along the lines suggested might have been attempted, but it does not follow that the federal policy that was adopted is vulnerable because a cooperative scheme on a legislative power basis was not tried first. Cooperative federalism may be consequential upon a lack of federal legislative power, but it is not a ground for denying it.[5]

There is no doubt that the Chief Justice's reasoning here accords with the existing Canadian constitutional precedents. But the teachers' argument was a particularly interesting one. It was in line with contemporary continental European thinking on the notion of federal comity and on the affirmative constitutional obligations of cooperation on the part of the different members of a federal polity. It is a pity that this reasoning was not picked up by the Canadian Supreme Court in its ruling.

The remaining three majority judges, speaking through Justice Ritchie's opinion, rested their conclusion in favour of the constitutionality of the federal act upon the federal government's general 'Peace, Order, and good Government' power in the light of the 'emergency' situation.[6] The two dissenting French-Canadians, Justices Beetz and de Grandpré, speaking through Beetz's dissenting opinion, addressed themselves to the same point. They denied that the federal government had established the existence of an 'emergency' situation so as to support the expanded interpretation of section 91 at the expense of the provinces' powers under section 92.

Two decisions of the Supreme Court of Canada were handed down at the end of 1977 in major federal-provincial conflicts. These lent support to the continuing complaint of Quebec and the English-speaking provinces against the extension of federal legislative competences under the BNA Act at the expense of the provinces – through decision of the Supreme Court!

The first decision involved a challenge by an accountant from Matane, Quebec to the constitutionality of a provincial board created by the Quebec government to license the operation of cable television companies within the province.

The second major decision involved a private oil corporation, Canadian Industrial Gas and Oil Ltd., and the government of the province of Saskatchewan. The company challenged the constitutionality of the provincial government's oil royalty tax system directed to the unexpected windfall profits made by the company as the beneficiary of the OPEC group's massive increases in world oil prices from 1973 onwards.

Both decisions involved split courts. The Quebec cablevision decision was rendered by a six to three majority, with Chief Justice Laskin writing the opinion of the court majority and all three Quebec judges dissenting. The other was rendered by a seven to two majority. Justice Martland wrote the majority opinion. Two of the three Quebec justices (Pigeon and Beetz) joined with him and the other majority judges; while Justice Dickson and the third Quebec justice (de Grandpré, since resigned from the court) dissented.

There was a tendency in the public comment upon these two decisions (rendered within one week of each other), to view both as confirming the existence of a profoundly centralist philosophy among the judicial majority on the Supreme Court, and to view the court accordingly as an instrument of the federal government in its own centralizing approach. Chief Justice Laskin took the unusual step of responding personally to the public criticisms of the two Supreme Court decisions.[7] He appeared to be particularly upset by the implication that the court and its judges were 'acting as spear-carriers for the Prime Minister.'[8] But the Chief Justice also hit out at a proposal advanced by, among others, one of the provincial premiers, that the provinces participate in the appointment of judges to the court.

Such criticisms are perhaps unwarranted attacks upon the independence of the current Supreme Court bench. The Privy Council rulings of the heyday of Watson and Haldane pointed to a decision the other way in each of the two cases here concerned, but half a century of jurisprudence since that time has created a heavy weight of precedents sanctioning expansion of federal government competences at the expense of the provinces. Almost all of the current members of the Supreme Court bench (including the present Chief Justice) have been appointed within the past decade. They could hardly have *carte blanche* to amend Ottawa's judicially created centralizing mandate. The court majority cannot be criticized for operating within the restrictions of constitutional precedent and in accordance with the accepted, judicially created constitutional rules of the past thirty years.

In the cablevision case, the federal government argued for exclusive federal competence over communications under section 91 of the BNA Act. The BNA Act of 1867 could hardly have foreseen our highly sophisticated and novel modes of communications and the problems of jurisdiction inevitably engendered by them. The federal government had of necessity to rely upon other quite limited and specific heads of section 91. These were of course directed to other purposes and needs, and so Ottawa had to argue for a progressive extension of those heads of power to meet the new forms of communication not envisaged in 1867. Such a generic interpretation would go beyond the canons of strict and literal interpretation of the constitution. But supreme courts exercising judicial review of a constitutional charter normally regard such extensions as within the competence of their office.

In 1932 the courts had had to reconcile with the 1867 division of legislative competences the power claimed by the federal government to implement an international treaty dealing with the then novel subject of radio communications. The *Radio* ruling[9] is normally linked with two other leading cases, the *Aeronautics* ruling of 1932[10] and the *Labour Conventions* ruling of 1937,[11] as a trilogy of authoritative judgments on the meaning and scope of the foreign affairs power under the Canadian constitution.

In the 1932 *Radio* case the Privy Council felt itself unable to reconcile federal government legislative implementation of an international treaty with the strict and literal meaning of section 132 of the BNA Act. It was not a British-made, 'British Empire' treaty but a treaty entered into by Canada in its new international capacity and in its own right. The ruling upheld the federal government legislation under the federal government's general 'Peace, Order, and good Government' power. The Privy Council refused to make generic extension of the federal government's section 132 powers to meet a novel problem falling clearly within the historical intent of the section. However, with Lord Dunedin writing its opinion, the Privy Council took the more debatable and controversial step of extending Ottawa's section 91 general power, at the expense of the provinces' section 92 powers, to meet the new situation. The opinion did not in any real way spell out the generic similarities to the existing federal powers in the communications area – for example, section 91(2) ('the Regulation of Trade and Commerce'), 91(5) ('Postal Service'), and 91(10) ('Navigation and Shipping').

In the cablevision case,[12] the Supreme Court majority ruled that the Quebec government had exceeded its constitutional authority in a 1972 statute. That law established provincial regulatory authority over cable television systems within the province by creating a provincial board and by requiring cable television companies operating in the province to be licensed by the board. A Matane, Quebec accountant, who had already been awarded one half of a cable television district in the lower St Lawrence valley by the Quebec board, wanted to take over the other half of the district which the Quebec board had already allocated to someone else. The Quebec government stressed the 'message' – what is communicated, and the fact that cable TV was intended primarily for public education; rather than the 'medium' – how the communication was made, and the technical modes of communicating the message.

Nevertheless, a major part of the province's substantive legal case rested upon the possibility of distinguishing legally between the mode of communication involved in cable television (distribution by telephone cable), and the mode of communication involved in the *Radio* case in 1932 (broadcasting by Hertzian waves). Quebec argued that the first was essentially local and therefore within section 92(16) provincial legislative competence, and thus avoided the need for a frontal assault upon or attempt to over-rule at this late stage the Privy Council's judgment in the *Radio* case. This was the argument adopted by the three dissenting Quebec judges in the opinion written by Justice Pigeon. He and his Quebec colleagues did not see any necessary complication if one distinguished cable television as local from radio broadcasting as federal (as held in 1932). Divided jurisdiction was, in their view, inherent in any federal system.

On the other hand, the six English-speaking judges, in their majority opinion written by Chief Justice Laskin, contended that cable television was part of an 'interrelated system of transmitting and receiving television signals, whether directly through air waves or through intermediate cable line operations ... Cable distribution enterprises ... rely on broadcasting stations, and their operations are merely a link in a chain which extends to subscribers who receive the programmes through their private receiving sets.'[13]

In finding broadcasting, including cable distribution, to consist of a unified system that was necessarily federal, Chief Justice Laskin declined to focus upon two aspects stressed by the dissenting judges, namely that the service involved in cable distribution was limited to intra-provincial subscribers, and that it was operated by a local concern. In the hearings before the Supreme Court the Quebec government's position had been supported by the governments of Ontario, Saskatchewan, Alberta, and British Columbia.

The Supreme Court gave a further ruling on the same day as the cablevision decision, in *Capital Cities Communications* v. CRTC.[14] In effect the court upheld the right of the federal Canadian Radio-Television and Telecommunications Commission to order cable television systems in Canada to delete commercials in programs emanating from US stations as a means of discouraging Canadian advertisers from buying broadcasting time in the United States. There was a six to three judgment, with the Chief Justice again writing the majority opinion and the three Quebec judges again dissenting in an opinion written by Justice Pigeon.

The Supreme Court dismissed a challenge by three Buffalo, New York television stations to the CRTC. Quebec, Ontario, Alberta, and British

Columbia had intervened in the case in support of the three Buffalo stations. The argument before the Supreme Court in this case, as in the main cablevision case, had attempted to distinguish and limit the 1932 *Radio* holding. It suggested that while the federal government might have exclusive jurisdiction over the receiving of television signals at the *antennae* of the cablevision companies, once received at those *antennae* federal legislative power should be exhausted. Any subsequent distribution of the signals, whether in the same or modified form, within a province, should be a matter of exclusive provincial concern.

In rejecting these arguments, the Chief Justice repeated his reasoning in the main cablevision case. There was a single undertaking throughout, and the switch to a different technology to bring the telecast to paying subscribers did not involve a switch from federal to provincial jurisdiction. He rejected 'technology of transmission as a ground for shifting constitutional competence.'[15]

The Supreme Court had decided one week earlier in the *Canadian Industrial Gas and Oil* case.[16] This involved the attempt by the NDP government of Saskatchewan to tax the unexpected windfall profits accruing to companies from the world energy crisis that followed on the OPEC group's massive increase in oil prices in 1973. When Canadian oil companies began to increase their own prices in response to the world price increases, the Saskatchewan government legislated in 1974 to provide that any increase in the price of Saskatchewan oil above the 1973 level should go to the Saskatchewan government and not to the oil companies.

The Saskatchewan government's measure no doubt partly reflected the aversion of a social democratic administration to the idea of unearned increments going to the oil companies in Canada simply as a result of the operation of world market conditions. The Saskatchewan government, in specifying its imposition as being a royalty, sought to tie it in to the undoubted provincial power over natural resources within the province. The government did not want the levy seen as an 'indirect' tax within the province which would be constitutionally prohibited by implication from section 92(2) of the BNA Act.

The decision in the *CIGOL* case was rendered by a seven to two majority, with Justice Martland writing the majority opinion and Justice Dickson writing a dissenting opinion on behalf of himself and the Quebec justice, de Grandpré. The majority ruled that the Saskatchewan mineral tax and royalty surcharges on crude oil, estimated to have yielded the province an extra 580 million dollars since 1974, were unconstitutional. They did not constitute 'direct taxation within the Province,' and therefore fell outside provincial legislative powers under section 92 of the BNA Act. Unlike a direct tax, it was not being paid by the corporation or producer against whom it was being levied, but was being passed on, like a wholesale or excise tax, to the eventual consumer.

As a further point, the majority considered that the levy was, in effect, an export tax, determining the price of a product beyond the Saskatchewan borders. As such, it reached international and inter-provincial trade and commerce, for ninety-eight per cent of Saskatchewan's oil was exported to eastern Canada or the United States. It thus constituted a provincial invasion of areas of federal legislative competence. Justice Dickson in his dissenting opinion rejected the argument that the Saskatchewan law was 'merely a colourable device for assuming control of extra-provincial trade.' He pointed out that the purchasers of the Saskatchewan oil would be paying the same price whether the tax existed or not.

The *CIGOL* case, unlike the cablevision and the cable TV commercials cases, did not raise direct Ottawa-Quebec conflicts as such. The joining by one of the Quebec judges, de Grandpré, with the other dissenter, Dickson, was perhaps more readily attributable to his corporate law expertise than to Quebec intellectual influences in the strict sense. The 1974 Saskatchewan law was paralleled by similar measures in Alberta, but the Alberta government – no doubt in part because, as a far wealthier province, it could afford to do so – exacted a much lower percentage of windfall profits from the oil companies and so avoided a legal challenge from them.

Nevertheless, the larger problem remained of the balance to be made between the provinces' competence over natural resources within the province and the federal government's powers of taxation. Where was one to establish the limits of the provinces' power over 'direct taxation within the Province' under section 92(2), in competition with the federal government's much more broadly defined section 91(3) tax power. Coming as it did only a week before the two cablevision decisions, the *CIGOL* decision was accepted, in the political and other public commentaries and criticisms, as confirming the existence of a profoundly centralist philosophy in the court's approach to federal-provincial conflicts over legislative competences. Three 1978 decisions against Saskatchewan seemed to provide further confirmation.

The Supreme Court decided by a unanimous, seven to nil vote, on 3 October 1978 – only fifteen days before the Saskatchewan general election – a case brought by Central Canada Potash Company Ltd. The court ruled unconstitutional the province of Saskatchewan's potash pro-rationing scheme whereby the province had regulated its potash industry since 1969. The court ruling was based on the argument that Saskatchewan was imposing an indirect tax and also interfering with inter-provincial and international trade.

On the same day, the Supreme Court also ruled unanimously, by a seven to nil vote, that the province of Saskatchewan must pay interest, estimated at many millions of dollars, on the money collected by its 1974 mineral tax and crude oil royalty legislation already struck down by the court as unconstitutional in its late 1977 decision in the *CIGOL* case.

Finally, on the same day, the Supreme Court again ruled unanimously, by a seven to nil vote, against an appeal by the Saskatchewan Power Corporation that would have given it supplies of natural gas at about twenty-five cents a thousand cubic feet instead of the current price of about $1. The court rejected the Saskatchewan Power Corporation's argument that the natural gas it was now entitled to buy from TransCanada Pipelines Ltd was not a straight sale but an exchange for gas it had earlier provided to TransCanada Pipelines.

Premier Blakeney of Saskatchewan, in the midst of his election campaign, reacted angrily to this trilogy of court decisions. He accused the federal government of 'trying to wrest control of resources from the provinces' by going through the court, and indicated that he would demand changes in the constitution at the up-coming constitutional conference. At the First Ministers' constitutional conference, in fact, the Premier charged that the court's decisions on constitutional matters favour the federal government because the judicial appointees of the federal government come with 'a set of predilections.'[17]

Premier Lougheed, whose pre-conference brief included a proposal for a constitutional panel of forty to fifty judges, echoed Blakeney's complaint. The brief noted that, while a key figure in the trilogy of Supreme Court decisions against Saskatchewan had been Justice Martland, the only Albertan on the court, 'it doesn't matter how judges are appointed, because after twenty years in Ottawa they all think alike.'[18] It now seems clear that Lougheed's 'constitutional court' trial balloon was only launched for debating reasons, to be abandoned for tactical compromises at a propitious moment. The real remedy would lie in an extension of the constitutional powers of the provinces under the BNA Act, and in their further refinement and clarification in section 92 of the BNA Act so as to reduce the scope for judicial interpretation and so render them fool-proof against any further, pro-Ottawa Supreme Court rulings.

There seemed to be a tactical shift, on the part of key provincial premiers like Blakeney and Lougheed, from changing the Supreme Court into a less determinedly 'federalist' body, to a new emphasis on rewriting sections 91 and 92 in favour of the provinces and on restating provincial legislative powers in contemporary terms and presumably *in extenso*. This would eliminate or reduce the scope for judicial review. Such a tactical shift is present also in the resistance by so many provincial premiers at this time – as demonstrated at the 1978 First Ministers' constitutional conference, and including Quebec, the western provinces, and possibly also Ontario – to the idea of an entrenched bill of rights. They see this as encouraging the Supreme Court further to interfere in political and social issues which, they believe, are rightfully determined by executive and legislative authority, rather than by judicial power. The premiers' claims, here, would seem to be a contemporary variant of the classical English constitutional principle of the sovereignty of Parliament, and the legal supremacy of the popularly elected legislature over the other organs of government.

At the time of the release of the federal government's 1978 constitutional proposals, a blow was being dealt by the Federal Court of Appeal to the protection for the 'French fact' at the federal level given by the Official Languages Act, 1969. The action stemmed from a festering dispute between francophone and anglophone air traffic controllers in Quebec. The invariably unilingual anglophone controllers apparently feared that they would be displaced by bilingual controllers if the use of French were permitted in air-ground communications within Quebec.

   This initially low-level labour relations dispute became a full-fledged linguistic quarrel. The Canadian Airline Pilots Association (CALPA) and the Canadian Air Traffic Controllers Association (CATCA) asked for a federal government ban on the use of French in air-ground communications and the exclusive use of English as the 'international language of aviation' – in the name of air traffic safety in Quebec and Canadian air space. An illegal strike of several days launched by these two essentially anglophone groups induced the federal Minister of Transport to issue, in August 1976, a federal Transport Ministry Order in effect forbidding the use of French in air-ground communications in Quebec.

   The Transport Ministry Order was challenged in the Federal Court of Canada by *l'Association des gens de l'air du Québec*, a Quebec-based francophone organization in opposition to CATCA. The Quebec association contended that the federal Order was discriminatory against francophone citizens and therefore illegal in terms of the federal Official Languages Act. In January 1977 Judge Marceau of the Federal Court, Trial Division, rejected the Quebec association claim.[19] On appeal to the Federal Court of Appeal, a three-man bench (Judges Pratte, Le Dain, and Hyde – the first a francophone), confirmed Judge Marceau's original decision, the judgment being rendered on 27 June 1978.[20]

Judge Pratte concluded that a language (in this case, French) can still be an official language even if, for reasons of security, its use is prohibited in certain exceptional circumstances; and that even if the ministerial order violated the Official Languages Act, it would not be illegal on that account since federal aviation laws had priority over the act. Judge Pratte indicated that he could not believe that Parliament, in proclaiming the equality of French and English in all the institutions of Parliament and of the government of Canada, had intended to limit the power of the federal Minister of Transport to decree regulations that he judged necessary to the security of air navigation.

The other judicial opinion filed in the Federal Court of Appeal by Judge Le Dain (Judge Hyde concurring with him), affirmed categorically that the Official Languages Act recognizes the official status of the two languages (French and English) and the strict right to use French, quite as much as English, in the institutions of the federal government. To the extent that the Minister of Transport's order refused the strict right to employ French in the division of the federal government responsible for assuring aerial control, it was irreconcilable with the act and entered into contradiction with it. Judge Le Dain added, however, that this contradiction did not invalidate the minister's order, on the ground that, in the absence of a legislative intention expressed in a particularly clear fashion, it could not be concluded that Parliament had wanted to subordinate its law on aviation to its law on the official languages.

The judgment of the Federal Court of Appeal, in sum, is an exercise in statutory construction. It is impossible to fault its logic in its application of statutory construction to constitutional interpretation. One can, however, question the general utility and relevance of such a narrowly legalistic view of constitutional rights and their limits. Did the Federal Court of Appeal assume that it, as an intermediate court only, should properly apply judicial self-restraint and leave policy issues involving language in aviation to Parliament or to the Supreme Court on appeal?

There is little doubt that the timing of the announcement of the judgment, with its apparent downgrading of the protection afforded by the Official Languages Act, resulted in damage to the federal government's position within Quebec. The President of *l'Association des gens de l'air du Québec* announced on 25 July 1978 that his association would not appeal the judgment to the Supreme Court of Canada. He indicated that the Federal Court's two decisions (in first instance, and on appeal) demonstrated that the Official Languages Act was inoperative in the association's sector of activity:

A Minister can decree in our particular domain – as a result, for example, of public pressures – a regulation which accords priority to English, and this regulation has priority of application over the Official Languages Act of the country. We thus understand, above all when it is repeated two times, that this instrument of the Canadian Official Languages Act is completely unsuitable and badly devised for the preservation of our language rights.

In all these conflicts, the federal executive has played a crucial role. The Supreme Court is, after all, a federal institution, and its occasions for making great constitutional pronouncements on federal-provincial conflicts, in which its alleged 'centralizing bias' has been demonstrated, depend to a large extent on prior initiatives of the federal government. The latter can decide whether or not to refer a particular matter to the court for advisory opinion on constitutionality, or whether or not to intervene in some constitutional litigation currently before the court and involving one or more provincial governments – and if so on what side.

Can the case be made for greater self-restraint on the part of the federal government in avoiding rushing to the court-house door, sword in hand, to do constitutional battle with provincial governments? Certainly some of the interventions of recent years against provincial governments in constitutional litigation were gratuitous, hasty, and ill-advised. They are not good federalism, for it is surely a violation of the principle of federal comity to intervene at law against a provincial government where no concrete, countervailing federal government interest is currently involved. Nor are they good constitutional problem-solving, particularly where federal-provincial negotiations have actually been proceeding at the time of Ottawa's recourse to the judicial process. The net effect of a favourable judicial decision on one's *legal* claims in the abstract – as World Court, as well as Canadian Supreme Court, jurisprudence shows – is to give the favoured party a sense of self-righteousness that impedes the obtaining of a reasonable compromise solution. It is a pity that Ottawa has not more often displayed the wise executive self-restraint on recourse to the Supreme Court that it has exercised on the two Quebec language laws. It resisted all the pressures by intransigent English-language pressure groups and political leaders to refer them to the Supreme Court for a hoped-for declaration of unconstitutionality.

If the case for more federal *executive* self-restraint seems clear and compelling, there is also a case for more federal *judicial* self-restraint – on the part of the Supreme Court judges, this time. Certainly, the Supreme Court, as a wholly federally nominated body, has sometimes seemed to be in a hurry to render judgment against the provinces, in situations where parallel judicial bodies in other countries consciously choose to make an ally of time and deliberately to delay their decision until political passions have cooled.

Perhaps the Supreme Court of Canada could help to minimize its own political difficulties in high 'political' cases by insisting on a more severe standard of constitutional 'interest' or standing to sue for private persons or interest groups before they are permitted to invoke constitutional issues before the court. Perhaps also – especially where the federal government intervenes – the court could more readily invoke the 'political questions' exception to its jurisdiction and refuse to consider matters more appropriately decided at the executive level of government, particularly where federal-provincial negotiations are already under way.

The ideal area for development of a more pluralistic federalism would thus appear to be less the judicial arena so dominant in federal problem-solving from the close of the nineteenth century until at least the early 1930s than the executive arena. Federal executive self-restraint in matters being negotiated, and positive action where appropriate, could produce constitutional change without formal amendment. Such an approach is posited upon quiet diplomacy in federal-provincial negotiation.

There are the First Ministers' conferences and the related ministers' conferences, and also the possibility of direct, bilateral negotiation between the federal government and an individual province. Even at the height of Ottawa-Quebec conflict after the election of the *Parti québécois* government such bilateral negotiations between the two capitals continued and the lines of direct communication were always maintained. We saw the seeming intransigence of both sides in the spring of 1978 over the federal plan to pay back specified federal revenue surpluses to the provinces in return for a uniform, across-the-board reduction of provincial sales tax – an unquestioned area of provincial competence. Yet in other areas substantial progress in joint, cooperative policy-making has been effected.

In the sales tax controversy, personality issues were also involved between the Quebec Finance Minister, Jacques Parizeau, and his federal analogue, Jean Chrétien. In retrospect, it probably would have been better for the federal government to have conceded gracefully to Quebec's counter-offer to the original federal proposals. The federal offer had been designed to stimulate the Canadian economy by putting money directly into the hands of the taxpayer. Quebec had proposed instead to remove the sales tax entirely from clothing, shoes and furniture – all Quebec industries currently needing a boost – but to limit the concession to those items alone. This difference degenerated into a more protracted conflict because of Ottawa's fear that to defer to Quebec's wishes would be seen by the English-speaking provinces as a concession to Quebec of some sort of special tax arrangement within Confederation. In fact, particularized arrangements of this nature to meet particularized local or regional economic needs are the life-blood of a working federal system, and it seems a pity that it required several months of newspaper controversy before a compromise embodying the essence of the Quebec counter-offer was finally accepted.

In regard to immigration, however, an area of concurrent federal and provincial legislative power under section 95 of the BNA Act, a compromise on competence was worked out quietly and effectively. Federal minister Bud Cullen, and his Quebec counterpart, Jacques Couture, agreed upon a special mixed committee of federal and provincial officials designed to ensure establishment of immigration levels for Quebec, in accordance with Quebec's needs and after consultation with Quebec. This agreement was no doubt facilitated by the relatively low public profiles and low-key personalities of the two ministers concerned, who concentrated on their technical responsibilities. A similar compromise between Ottawa and Quebec has at least been under discussion since the much-resented Supreme Court decision in the Quebec cablevision case at the end of 1977. Progress towards understanding in this area has no doubt been slower because of the existence of the judicial decision adverse to Quebec's case.

This mode of federal problem-solving through administrative arrangement between the two levels of government through direct negotiation remains, however, one of the most hopeful approaches to constitutional change. It is in the full spirit of what used to be called, in the early 1960s, cooperative federalism. Pending some break in the longstanding impasse over amendment machinery for the federal constitution, this is the best solution possible. Any fundamental constitutional changes depend on the existence of a prior national consensus. In the meantime, we have a pragmatic, gradualist approach to constitutional change through the development of special administrative glosses upon the original constitutional charter – an imaginative and constructive arrangement, building ultimately on the idea of federal comity.

What remain are more fundamental philosophical questions concerning the *raison d'être* for judicial review of the constitution within a plural state such as Canada. Do the judicial rules continue to make good sense as community problem-solving techniques when applied to great issues involving direct federal-provincial confrontations?

The Canadian Supreme Court has perhaps now become – *faute de mieux*, and without necessarily seeking such a rôle – a legislating, policy-making body for federal-provincial conflicts. Should it not prudently arm itself with some of the techniques of judicial self-restraint applied by other courts, the US Supreme Court and the West German Federal Constitutional Court, for example? Is any major public interest involved in the complaint by an oil company that its 'constitutional rights and freedoms' were being denied by the Saskatchewan royalty tax on windfall profits accruing from the OPEC countries' 1973 actions? It is again surely straining a point to imply that the public interest necessitated a court ruling on the claimed constitutional liberty of a private entrepreneur in Quebec – who had had already been awarded a license for half a cablevision operation region by the Quebec licensing authority – to take over the remaining half, to his own direct commercial gain.

As with the 'Old Court' that dominated US Supreme Court jurisprudence up to President Roosevelt's changes in court personnel after 1937, private commercial interests may have been permitted too easily to call in aid the constitutional 'rules of the game,' with no major and immediate public interest being involved. Considerable incidental harm may have been done to Canadian federalism at a peculiarly difficult period in our national history.

Could not the Supreme Court of Canada do what the US and West German courts have done in similar cases, and insist upon a very strict definition of the constitutional 'interest' (standing to sue) of private parties in great constitutional issues and also make an ally of time by not moving to decision prematurely? In the Quebec cablevision case, it was public knowledge that diplomatic negotiations were proceeding between Ottawa and Quebec directed to a rational compromise on the problem.

Even more, could not the federal government show more sensitivity to the Supreme Court's predicament when the court is called upon for judicial decision on problems in which the legal elements are limited or marginal? The government could certainly use its right of intervention upon constitutional issues raised by private interest groups before the court to counsel the court on the merits of delaying any decisions until any federal-provincial negotiations on those same issues should be completed.

Timely changes of this character, involving court practice and federal executive self-restraint, could do much to shield the Supreme Court from public criticisms and calls for reform or restructuring of the court. These criticisms come from respected political leaders not normally considered foes of the court or of judicial review of the constitution in general.

9
Ottawa's New Initiatives

In 1977 Ottawa appointed a Task Force on Canadian Unity, and began to plan an innovative two-stage approach to the rewriting of the constitution, once again taking the initiative in the adaptation of our federal system. After the failure of the Victoria Charter of 1971 the federal government had apparently concluded that no amendment of the constitution involving changes of the BNA Act could be expected in the immediate future. It decided upon a policy of constitutional *attente*, and directed its energies to specific problems of federal-provincial relations and their settlement on a basis of negotiation and reciprocity.

The election of the *Parti québécois* government in 1976 brought a flurry of activity in English-speaking Canada – most of it characterized by enthusiasm rather than by research and analysis. The federal government no doubt recognized the logical contradiction in presenting proposals for constitutional amendment to a Quebec government officially committed to leaving the federal system altogether. Perhaps Ottawa also reasoned that it was more sensible to make an ally of time, and to wait and see what the separatist position of the *Parti québécois* really meant in federal-provincial negotiations.

There was no immediate federal government reaction to the election by way of constitutional proposals to appease Quebec's claims or even to steal the Quebec separatists' constitutional thunder. The first major Ottawa initiative seems to have come, reluctantly and belatedly, to forestall opposition charges of federal government inaction.

The Task Force on Canadian Unity was formed by the federal government in the late summer of 1977. The formation of Premier Davis' Advisory Committee on Confederation and the holding of a large public conference on Confederation in Toronto financed by the Davis government had threatened to steal the rôle of constitutional spokesman for English-speaking Canada from the federal government.

The formation of the federal commission was delayed for some weeks by the search for French-Canadian members with respectable nationalist credentials to serve on the commission. The two finally selected, Solange Chaput-Rolland and Gérald Beaudoin, turned out to be among the most interesting and productive members of the commission. The two co-presidents, Jean-Luc Pépin and John Robarts, had impressive political backgrounds. Pépin had been a Liberal cabinet minister and Robarts Conservative Premier of Ontario throughout the 1960s. The Premier had been a key figure in the *entente cordiale* between Quebec and Ontario when relations between Quebec and Ottawa were often strained. Robarts was a lawyer by profession, Beaudoin a constitutional law professor, and Pépin originally a professor of political science; none of the other members had any particular claims to constitutional knowledge or expertise.

The commission also suffered from a lack of a genuinely non-partisan image, and this situation was not helped when one of its members, John Evans, president of the University of Toronto, resigned in March 1978 to accept a Liberal candidacy for the next federal election. Its executive director, Reed Scowen, resigned in May 1978 to accept a Liberal candidacy in a Quebec provincial by-election. Yet the major royal commissions (federal and provincial) of recent years on Canadian constitutional matters – the federal Bilingualism and Biculturalism Commission of the 1960s and the Quebec Gendron Commission – have not been predominantly 'expert' in their composition. They have not consciously sought to represent all political parties. The political impact of their recommendations has tended to depend on their intrinsic merit.

The Pépin-Robarts Commission mandate focussed on three general tasks: to support, encourage, and make known public and private efforts on behalf of national unity; to contribute the commission's own opinions; and to advise the federal government on matters having to do with national unity. The term 'national unity' allows many different interpretations. Like most royal commissions before it, this one ventured upon an exhausting cross-country series of public hearings at which it invited comments and suggestions from the general public. Most of these public reactions contributed little that was new or profound, and some were unpleasantly pejorative.

Yet there was solid, technically based comment from constitutional specialists and politicians, offering a cross-section of national opinion on federalism in general and on Quebec in particular. The commission had neither the time (with an original mandate of twelve months, later extended to the end of 1978) nor the staff to undertake extensive research. It seemed inevitable, because of the conflicting claims presented and the desire to present some remedies, that it would recommend changes in the BNA Act and the federal system as a whole.

Simultaneously with the work of the commission the federal government had its own civil-service task force on the constitution. Working under the direction of the minister in charge of federal-provincial relations, Marc Lalonde, it maintained its review of constitutional matters which had never been dropped in spite of the failure of the Victoria Charter. There had been suggestions that delays in announcing progress of this task force were linked to the federal election then expected in the spring of 1978. But when the federal government finally released the first report of the group, a White Paper entitled *A Time for Action – toward the renewal of the Canadian Federation*, in June 1978, it seemed anxious to regain control of constitutional change. This field was being preempted, *faute de mieux*, by various provincial premiers, the federal Conservative party, and a plethora of special interest associations and private pressure groups, all bringing forward hastily developed and often inadequately researched proposals. The government linked its new proposals to previous federal-provincial discussions, the constitutional innovations proposed being essentially reformulations or extensions of the 1971 proposals.

A Time for Action nevertheless appeared to be a program for action rather than a set of recommendations for constitutional amendment. This is not intended in a pejorative sense nor is it meant to imply that it was drafted as an election platform. It simply indicates that the propositions were all formulated at a very high level of generality and abstraction, without tethering details.

We would need further refinement and elaboration before any of these primary principles could be implemented. The paper included an extension of the Victoria Charter project of involving the provinces in the process of federal judicial appointments. The latter's very complicated and (some might say) cumbersome machinery for federal consultation with the provinces remained, without the federal government giving up its sole power of appointment.

In its 'renewed Federation' proposals, Ottawa repeated the essence of the 1971 proposal on the Supreme Court, though limiting itself to the statement that it 'would seem only appropriate that the [Provinces] should have a voice when appointments to the Court are made by the Government of Canada.'

The federal government, however, suggested for the first time a 'new legislative body, the House of the Federation ... as a replacement for the Senate.' Essential features of the new house would be the 'recognition of a rôle for the provinces in the selection of its members and provision for proportionately greater representation to the eastern and western parts of the country, with substantial adjustment to ensure adequate representation for Western Canada.'

Note the federal government's disposition to move in an area that (except perhaps for provincial representation in the Senate) would be wholly within federal legislative competence under the BNA Act (No. 2), 1949, and therefore not running any risk of provincial attempts at veto. The absence of specifics allowed Ottawa to avoid the rigidities of the 1971 court proposal and to sidestep neatly the hidden legal pitfalls in the proposals advanced by various provincial governments for a *Bundesrat*-style upper house.

The rest of the constitutional package covered familiar ground, and to many people reflected as much the vestiges of Cartesianism in Prime Minister Trudeau's personal philosophy,[1] as the felt need to respond to the challenge of the Lévesque government. There is a long and detailed recitation of the postulated 'deficiencies of the Constitution' – *inter alia*, that it is 'scattered throughout a large number of different statutes,' that 'its spirit is not described and its nature and objectives are not specified,' that 'its language is obscure and anachronistic, its style plodding and uninspiring,' and that it is 'of little educative value' with 'little to inspire the pride, solidarity, magnanimity and serious commitment required for the pursuit of a national ideal.' There is reference again to the 'lack of any declaration of the basic rights and freedoms of Canadians,' to the fact that 'the status of the Supreme Court is not set forth in the Constitution,' and the fact that 'the procedure for the amendment of the Constitution is not adequately defined in our constitutional enactments.'

Such criticisms could be applied, almost *in toto*, to the constitution of Great Britain, and also, in part, to such varied constitutions as those of the United States and Israel. Yet all of these, as well as the Canadian constitution, are and have been genuinely operational. These constitutions, then, are normative and not nominal, where so many more perfect philosophers' blueprints of constitutions today remain in so many countries law-in-books and are never translated into law-in-action.

The point, surely, is not that we would not have a better constitution for Canada by meeting all these criticisms; but simply that we have managed to get along very well without any such changes, and that they are hardly priority issues today, either in Quebec or in English Canada. The irony is that 'patriation' of the BNA Act and insertion of an 'entrenched' bill of rights have become priority issues devised by English Canada and used by a French-Canadian Prime Minister as a response to Quebec demands that ignore these issues. These proposals should, I think, be appraised on their merits and considered as English-Canadian demands whose impact, if any, will be in English Canada.

In the proposed 'entrenched' federal Charter of Rights and Freedoms the crucial question (for Quebec) of language was dealt with by a statement of the federal government's 'profound conviction that the citizens of Canada, whether they speak English or French, should be able, in those situations where numbers warrant, to receive basic government services and schooling for their children in their language. The Charter would be intended to provide a permanent constitutional guarantee that fair and reasonable treatment will always prevail.'[2]

All this is more useful politically than making categorical prescriptions concerning the language situation before Quebec or Canada as a whole have reached a consensus on the policy to be adopted. The question remains, however: if consensus on the subject has not been achieved should one be deliberately vague in the constitution rather than say nothing at all? If the language issue is left out perhaps an 'entrenched' bill of rights will take us little beyond the Bill of Rights of 1960 in the constitutional protection of civil liberties. It will probably not contribute to a resolution of the current dilemma of French Canada.

The federal package discusses the distribution of legislative powers, but, wisely, does not propose any immediate solutions. It rejects some current provincial proposals for a 'massive shift of powers from the federal government to the provinces'; but it recognizes both a need for some exchange of powers between the provinces and the federal government and also the merits of an extension of concurrent jurisdictions [with] the recognition that one order of government or the other has primary jurisdiction in specific areas. These questions were deliberately left to the provincial government for future examination.

There is reference to a need for study of the 'institutions of the executive of our central government.' It starts out as a plea for reducing to written form certain unspecified conventional aspects of the constitution; but seems, intriguingly, to offer the promise of new proposals for the future. Is there a hint of a shift from a parliamentary-style executive to something closer to the American system that has in practice emerged increasingly in Canada?

The clear breakthrough in the package is Ottawa's admission that constitutional law is as much process as it is substantive principles in themselves.

The federal government here invokes for constitutional law development a methodology developed and applied in international law-making. The method includes the reduction of a large problem into its smaller constituent units; the use of time, so that the more immediately tractable problems are dealt with first; and the determination of one's priorities for problem-solving according to one's resources, including one's jurisdictional power. In practical terms this meant dividing constitutional law-making into different phases, and determining those matters to be allocated to the first phase on the basis of whether or not they fell wholly within federal legislative power.

Thus in phase I, which the federal government felt should be completed by 1 July 1979, the federal government placed the Supreme Court, the 'House of the Federation,' the federal executive, the preamble to the constitution, and the new 'entrenched' Bill of Rights. All of these are subjects within exclusive federal legislative power under the BNA Act (No. 2) of 1949. They therefore do not require, under constitutional law or convention, any prior provincial assent to federal government action. The federal government pledged itself to 'consult with the provincial governments ... and to seek to work out proposals for action by Parliament which would have maximum support from the governments of the provinces.' Any such consultation, however, would be a matter of courtesy only and not of right. Any attempt at veto by one or more of the provinces would be neither effective nor an excuse or justification for delay on Ottawa's part.

The remaining matters in the package require, by constitutional convention, federal-provincial cooperation and assent. These were consigned to phase II of the process, since presumably requiring more time for completion. This left a target date for completion of the second phase, and for adoption of a new constitution as a whole, of 1 July 1981.

Prime Minister Trudeau released in June 1978 – a week after *A Time for Action* set out his general philosophy and time-table for the renewal of the Canadian federation – the text of a Constitutional Amendment Bill (Bill C-60). It contained the institutional structure, ground rules, and legislative guide-lines for a new federal constitution in place of the BNA Act of 1867. The Prime Minister indicated that he intended to refer the bill to a joint committee of the Senate and House of Commons, and to discuss it with the provincial governments at a forthcoming First Ministers conference.

In accordance with the political strategy for a two-phase approach outlined in the white paper, the new Constitutional Amendment Bill concentrated on matters wholly within the federal government's law-making competence under the BNA Act (No. 2) of 1949. This was a clear indication that the

promised discussion of the proposed changes with the provincial governments would not become an excuse for federal inaction if unanimous or
substantial provincial acquiescence were withheld or even unduly delayed.

The Constitutional Amendment Bill, 1978, essayed a number of tactical
innovations in the approach to constitutional change. There was to be a
staged, two-step approach rather than one single, general act of constitution-
making. There was a time schedule or term of years fixed for completion of
the process, with a definite cut-off date. Some priority was established between the different areas or subjects of possible change. And, finally, the
decision was made by the federal government to act upon its own initiative
rather than to wait indefinitely upon the attainment of some more general-
ized, inter-governmental consensus.

In terms of comparative legal science, it is difficult to fault this approach as
a legal method. Comparative constitutional-law history demonstrates that
the comprehensive exercise of constituent power is normally attainable only
when a popular consensus supervenes upon some great political event – a
social or economic revolution, for example, or a great military victory, or
even a military disaster. In all other periods, the problem-oriented, step-by-
step approach has normally been the most fruitful method. This method
implies due attention to the time factor and to the establishment of immediate objectives for constitutional change within determinate time periods. It
also implies a system of ranking priorities for change, involving assessment
of the possibility and social costs of the different, alternative, and sometimes
competing projects for change. In any such assessment one must consider
whether one has effective control, oneself, of the instruments and machinery of change, so that one can really influence the timing of change – and act
alone if necessary.

The practical dilemma of the federal government in approaching constitu-
tional change is clear. Unless and until the issue of separatism is resolved in
Quebec, it is not possible to speak of any Quebec consensus as to 'What
Quebec really wants' in the constitutional domain.

It is hardly propitious for the federal government to venture upon any
general act of constitution-making in such a highly conditional situation. Yet
not to act at all invites the charge – which inevitably becomes ammunition
for the separatist cause – that Ottawa is irrevocably wedded to the constitutional *status quo* and unwilling to make any changes to meet Quebec's special
claims – whatever they might be. In the Constitutional Amendment Bill,
1978, the government limited itself to matters it considered to be wholly
within federal competence and capable of being amended by simple act of
the federal Parliament. The federal government thereby demonstrated both

its openness to constitutional change and its practical disposition to retain the constitutional initiative itself by carrying this particular set of proposals through to completion 'with all deliberate speed' and by its own effort if need be.

Assorted English-speaking premiers at Regina in August 1978 objected that it was 'unconstitutional' for the federal government to act in this matter – 'unilaterally' – without waiting on a prior consensus of all of the provinces (including Quebec). (The *Parti québécois* government assisted jovially, and perhaps not merely with tongue in cheek, in the discussions of the proposals for constitutional change *within* the existing federal system, in spite of its own formal commitment to separatism and constitutional change only *outside* Confederation.) The premiers' objections seemed both politically unfair and to display a general lack of understanding of the basic science of constitution-making.

The premiers complained that the federal government was limiting itself to matters within federal constitutional competence and escpecially to federal institutional change (involving the Senate and the Supreme Court), but not touching the division of powers between the federal government and the provinces (involving sections 91 and 92 of the BNA Act of 1867). The premiers seemed to be inviting the federal government to open a Pandora's box of jurisdictional squabbles which would require a full federal and provincial consensus – and this before Quebec had decided its constitutional future, within or without confederation. Bowing to these provincial criticisms, however, the Prime Minister announced in mid-September 1978 that he was prepared to negotiate with the provinces on both division of legislative competence and changes in existing federal institutions.

One question remains, however. What is the validity of the premiers' claim to be able to veto federal proposals for constitutional change on matters coming under Ottawa's sole jurisdiction as to constitutional amendment, in terms of the BNA Act (No. 2) of 1949? Why is it assumed that provincial premiers have the constitutional right to speak on behalf of the people of their provinces in matters wholly within federal jurisdiction and competence under the BNA Act of 1867? What does that do to the prior constitutional rights of the federal members of Parliament elected from any province?

There seems to be a misunderstanding of the basic theory of the modern federal state that, if consistently applied and carried to its logical conclusion, would take us right back to the constitutional theory of the Holy Roman Empire or, in the extreme case, the Kingdom of Poland of the *liberum veto* era. Rather than see the federal system disintegrate into a conclave of perpetually warring princes, it would seem preferable to consider submitting the federal proposals for constitutional change to a direct exercise in constituent power. Perhaps a popularly elected constituent assembly would be premature now (though perhaps not, later), for the same reasons advanced in the case of a general act of constitution-making. But popular referenda might be held in all provinces simultaneously – a current federal government suggestion for which the premiers have shown a remarkable lack of enthusiasm. Their attitude is hardly surprising since referenda would deprive them of the shreds of their claim to a popular mandate to speak on behalf of the people of their provinces in constitutional matters falling solely within federal juris-diction under the BNA Act.

10

The Constitutional Amendment Bill, 1978

The Constitutional Amendment Bill, 1978, limits itself essentially to the area of federal government constitutional competence and concentrates on three major types of amendment. The first category involves a new and more consciously literary – poetic, if you wish – preamble to the constitution in place of the dull and prosaic rendition of 1867. It manages in high-level, abstract, and also conveniently general terms to encompass both the 'deux nations' theory of Canadian federalism and the reality of an increasingly multi-cultural Canadian society. The category also includes restyling the Governor-General as Canadian head of state (sections 42–8); formally providing for the office of Prime Minister and the institution of the federal cabinet (sections 49–54); and institutionalizing the practice of the federal-provincial First Ministers' conference (sections 97–9).

These proposed amendments would do no more, in the federal government's view, than reduce to positive constitutional law what are already long-standing constitutional customs and conventions. They would add nothing significantly new but would all be brought together in one document – in a general constitutional restatement.

It must have been a surprise to the federal government to find that the sections on the office of Governor-General were bitterly contested as somehow reducing the constitutional prerogative powers of the Queen or 'abolishing the monarchy in Canada.' This criticism drew strength, no doubt, from the almost simultaneous release of the Prime Minister's bill and the report 'Towards a new Canada,' released by the Canadian Bar Association's Committee on the Constitution. The latter recommended on 'the Executive and Head of State': 'The Queen should be recognised as Head of the Commonwealth.' 'A Canadian should be Head of State ... The Head of State should be chosen for a fixed term by a majority vote in the House of Commons.'

This particular set of proposals – only one among 133 recommendations by the committee – so upset the members of the Bar Association, assembled in their national annual general meeting in Halifax in August 1978, that they voted to refer the report to the provincial branches for study – a euphemism understood to signify that the whole report was being consigned to limbo. The Lieutenant-Governor of Nova Scotia had earlier declined to attend the Bar meeting, the refusal apparently being linked to the 'abolition of the monarchy' issue.

By contrast, the Prime Minister's bill seems subtle and cautious, and deliberately eschews breaking new constitutional ground: 'There shall be an officer for Canada styled the Governor General of Canada, who shall be appointed by the Queen by letters patent under the Great Seal of Canada ... and who shall represent the Queen in Canada and exercise for her the prerogatives, functions and authority belonging to her in respect of Canada by the Constitution of Canada or otherwise pursuant to law' (section 42).

Is there anything in this recitation and in the related sections 43 to 48 that goes beyond the conventional (customary) law of the constitution as to the existing state of the prerogative powers of the Queen in relation to Canada? As a matter of legal drafting, surely not! Nevertheless, the provincial premiers (including M Lévesque), meeting in Regina in August 1978, issued a communiqué at the close of the conference *inter alia* opposing 'constitutional changes that substitute for the Queen as ultimate authority a Governor General whose appointment and dismissal would be solely at the pleasure of the federal cabinet.' (Quebec's Minister for Inter-Governmental Affairs, Claude Morin, in a fashion even defended the monarchy at Regina.) The premiers further declared that it was 'doubtful whether the federal government has the legal authority to proceed unilaterally with proposed changes to ... the rôle of the monarchy. In any event, it would clearly be wrong for them to undertake unilateral action ... without provincial support.'[1]

These criticisms of this particular part of the Constitutional Amendment Bill were echoed in the Special Joint Committee of the Senate and the House of Commons on the Constitution of Canada. The committee voted nineteen to eleven, on the motion of a Conservative member, Flora MacDonald, that these particular sections of the bill be referred (together with other sections of the bill having to do with the reconstitution of the Senate) to the Supreme Court for advisory opinion on their constitutionality. Liberal senators joined with Conservative and NDP House members to make up the majority.

Prime Minister Trudeau, for his part, denied any intention of changing the rôles of the Governor-General or the Crown, his purpose being simply to inscribe in the proposed charter the situation as it already existed. So the federal government, while agreeing to make a constitutional reference to the Supreme Court as to the sections touching on the Senate, stood firm against any Supreme Court reference in relation to the sections of the new bill dealing with the Governor-General. The reference to the Supreme Court for advisory opinion as to the Senate was formally made by the federal government at the end of November 1978.

In a second and somewhat analogous category falls the proposed new Charter of Rights and Freedoms (sections 5–29). This is to be binding on the federal government as soon as it should become law but only on the provinces if and when they should affirmatively decide to 'opt in' to these provisions of the new charter. This aspect of the Constitutional Amendment Bill represents, no doubt, the French aspects – Cartesian and logical – of Prime Minister Trudeau's constitutional thinking. We can see the desire to reduce to abstract written charter-form parts of the common-law constitutional law of Canada contained in the 'received' English constitutional precedents and in the more than forty years of judicial decisions of a succession of strong judges on the Supreme Court of Canada – among these, Chief Justice Duff and Justice Ivan Rand.

There are new elements – notably the provisions on language rights which include a postulated new right to education in the language of one's choice (whether French or English) in the province (section 21). These new proposals could cause direct conflict with the provinces since they, *prima facie*, tread on areas of provincial legislative authority and, in the language of education sections at least, run counter to both Bill 22 and Bill 101. However, they are reconciled with political realities and rendered politically palatable by that 'opting in' stipulation that does not make them binding in provincial law unless and until the province concerned agrees thereto.

We should also note that it is today almost *de rigeur* in constitution-making exercises to include a bill of rights. We have seen the movement from a judicially developed and enforced unwritten bill of rights, through the statutory Bill of Rights of 1960, to proposals for an entrenched Bill of Rights. Perhaps this should be welcomed as an essentially modern element in our constitutionalism.

The real thrust of the Constitutional Amendment Bill, 1978, is contained in the institutional proposals. Most notable are the proposed changes in the Supreme Court of Canada and its composition and organization, and the proposals involving the replacement of the Senate by a new House of the Federation.

At first sight the proposals on the Supreme Court (sections 101–15) reflect simply the constitutional 'tidying up' involved in the inclusion in the constitution itself of what is now constitutional custom and convention or statutory law. I am not sure that much is changed by 'entrenching' the Supreme Court in the new constitution of Canada. There is not much gained by entrenching the 'special' representation for Quebec – increased from three to four judges (section 104) in a court whose total membership is increased from nine to eleven (section 102).

Indeed there is something new and not necessarily desirable in making express stipulations as to other, non-Quebec 'regional' representation on the court (section 104). Many may think that the past statutory provision for a 'special' (one-third) proportion of Quebec judges on the Supreme Court was a necessary and inevitable concession to French-Canadian nationalism. But they may also feel that the entrenching of a parallel principle of quotas for the other provinces represents a misunderstanding of the nature and character of the judicial office – apart from the catering to regional parochialism thereby involved.

A 'representative' judge is surely *parti pris* from the moment of his appointment: to paraphrase Sir Edward Coke, a judge should be representative of no man, but be under God and the Law. This feature seems to have been intended as a political gesture to provincial premiers, one of whom, at least, had claimed it as a constitutional right in his brief to the Pépin-Robarts Commission. The same might also be said of the elaborately contrived, unnecessarily bureaucratic, and constitutionally inelegant provisions for consulting provincial Attorneys-General on appointments to the Supreme Court of Canada (section 106). This latter was also proposed in the Victoria Charter of 1971; but the 1978 bill also requires the submission of all Supreme Court nominations to the new House of the Federation for confirmation (section 107). Thus there seems absolutely no need to consult the provincial Attorneys-General. Indeed this would add complexity and delays, and inevitably screen out the more sparkling judicial personalities – such as Duff, Rand, Laskin, and Pigeon – of our time.

In one respect new stipulations on the Supreme Court are a welcome advance on the present constitutional arrangements. Public discussion (even informal) of a particular candidate for the court – his legal qualifications, his intellectual outlook, and his philosophy of law – should overcome or neutralize the criticisms that have often followed a judicial appointment: a particular judge is too 'centralizing' in his approach to federal-provincial conflicts or else anti-civil-libertarian in his judicial philosophy. These issues should at least be discussed *before* confirmation.

Bill C-60 would of course preserve the Supreme Court in terms of basic jurisdiction and internal organization. The court would remain a court of general jurisdiction with – in addition to its constitutional domain – the power of final appellate review of common-law cases coming from supreme courts of the English-speaking provinces and of cases coming from Quebec courts involving the Quebec Civil Code. The temptation has thus been resisted of instituting a special constitutional court on the European model. The bill eschews even the possibility of such a specialized tribunal for federal-provincial constitutional conflicts and for federal constitutional law purposes more generally.

The Molgat-MacGuigan Report of 1972 had recommended that the provinces have the right to withdraw appeals in matters of strictly provincial law (which would certainly include regular common law and civil law appeals) from the Supreme Court of Canada and to vest final decision in such matters in their own provincial courts. This would apply to federal court jurisdiction that voluntarist, 'opting in /opting out,' principle that has been raised in the language rights provisions of the proposed Charter of Rights and Freedoms. No doubt only Quebec might feel inclined to 'opt out' of the Supreme Court's jurisdiction over private law appeals. Yet such an 'opting out' power conferred on the provinces might eventually confine the Supreme Court to constitutional matters. This would certainly clarify and simplify judicial selection which is now cluttered by the need to find judges who are both 'constitutional judges' and professionally competent to handle common law and civil law matters. Presumably, however, the strictly legal justification for having three of nine judges come from Quebc, as now required, would disappear if the court's jurisdiction over Quebec civil law appeals were lost. Correspondingly, the more the court became, *de facto*, a constitutional court, the more one would have to attend to what continental European jurists call the political 'legitimacy' of constitutional review by a court and to the claims to 'legitimacy' on the part of the individual judges themselves.

The proposed new House of the Federation (sections 62–70) would be the most important constitutional change. The new house would have the right to confirm or reject federal appointments to the Supreme Court of Canada (section 107) and to federal administrative bodies, federal Crown corporations and the like (section 70). The new house would have a virtual suspensive veto of up to two months over all bills enacted by the House of Commons, including revenue and tax bills (section 67). A suspensive veto is certainly less than the powers of the present Senate. However, the present Senate's powers have, for most practical purposes, today lapsed into desuetude or disappeared through long-time custom and convention. The new House of the Federation, with an electoral mandate of some sort, would no doubt expect to exercise to the full its right to criticize and delay House of Commons measures.

Complex legislative drafting and administrative application will be necessary to implement one aspect of the notion of two linguistic communities referred to in the preamble of the new bill. Section 69 states that bills 'of a special linguistic significance' are to require a double majority – a majority of the English-speaking and of the French-speaking members – for adoption in the House of the Federation. Other legislation will require only a simple majority for passage.

The most novel aspects of the House of the Federation are the provisions for the selection of its members. These provisions (sections 62 to 65) establish a house of 118 members, thirty-two from the four Atlantic provinces, thirty-six from the four western provinces, one each from the two northern territories, and twenty-four each from Ontario and Quebec.

This represents no concession to those Quebec claims for equality of representation for Quebec and English Canada in the Senate. It does involve a relative increase in the representation of the western provinces over that at present specified under section 22 of the BNA Act. This particular part of the proposals on the House of the Federation might fall outside Ottawa's constitutional power of unilateral action under the BNA Act (No. 2) of 1949. It might thus require the concurrence of the other sections of the country (the Atlantic provinces, Ontario, and Quebec) presumably adversely affected thereby.

The federal government had earlier indicated that it was satisfied with the validity of the 'Senate' as well as the other sections of the 1978 bill, and that it had the necessary jurisdiction to adopt them by simple act of the federal Parliament. There was, however, sharp criticism by the provincial premiers at their Regina meeting in August 1978; and the Senate-House Special Joint Committee on the Constitution voted nineteen to eleven (with opposition house members combining with senators of all parties to make the majority), that the 'Senate' and 'monarchy' sections of the bill should be referred to the Supreme Court. The federal government responded by announcing that it would, in fact, refer the 'Senate' sections – though not the others – to the court for an advisory opinion on their constitutionality.

The real change, however, lies in the plan to abolish the present monopoly power of the Prime Minister to appoint persons to the Senate when vacancies occur in its ranks through retirement or death. Instead there would be a complicated system of indirect election. One half of the total number of members from each province would be selected by the lower house of the federal Parliament, and the other half selected by the legislature of the province concerned (section 63). The federal selections for all provinces are to be made by the federal lower house immediately after each federal general election; the provincial selections are to be made by the provincial legislature concerned immediately after each provincial general election. Since there are ten provinces, and since the provinces invariably hold their general elections at different times from each other and from the federal government, this would mean eleven different partial elections to the House of the Federation in any four-year period. Indeed, if any one of the eleven governments should call elections early (say, through the collapse of a minority government) there would then be further partial elections. The new upper house will thus take on the character of a merry-go-round with a more or less continuing change or renewal of its membership. There are further detailed provisions for the selection, through indirect election, of the membership for each province in the house. Current members of the federal Commons or the provincial legislatures are disqualified under section 64(1). The canons of constitutional propriety would presumably also disqualify federal and provincial civil servants in the absence of an express constitutional permission. Various provincial premiers, in pressing the West German *Bundesrat* model, seemed to be seeking a dual rôle for themselves, their cabinet and party colleagues, and key civil service advisers, as members of a new federal upper house. This would be denied, it seems.

Prime Minister Trudeau has also clearly rejected another aspect of the provinces' *'Bundesrat* caper' – the notion of a provincial government monopoly to appoint all the members of what would, in effect, become a provincial government 'delegation' to the house. Section 64(2) stipulates that the system of indirect election after each general election, federal or provincial, is to be applied on a proportional representation basis according to the percentage of party votes in each province in the election. This is the first application of proportional representation in the Canadian federal system. The idea has occasionally been put forward as a means of correcting apparent voter 'alienation' in various sections of the country. The first-past-the-post voting system operates in single-member, geographically based electoral constituencies at the federal level; in Quebec and various western provinces this has often produced virtually a one-party slate in the province's federal members.

One wonders why Prime Minister Trudeau did not take the next step. He had rejected the provincial premiers' anachronistic demands for the right to appoint all the members of delegations to the new upper house. Why did he not then provide for direct, popular election to the upper house (as in the

United States and Australia); and direct, popular election on the basis of proportional representation within provincial boundaries (as in Australia)?

If there is to be a reform of the existing upper house, it should be a genuine 'reform'; and the trend in enlightened constitutionalism has been away from appointment and indirect elections in favour of direct, popular election – which alone can confer political legitimacy today.

In the Explanatory Document accompanying the Constitutional Amendment Bill, 1978, it is suggested that direct election to an upper house 'can work in a congressional system based on the separation of powers, such as that of the United States,' but not, by inference, in a parliamentary federal system. The possibility of a constitutional deadlock between an elected federal upper house and an elected federal lower house – such as occurred in Australia in 1975 – is avoided in the bill. There could be, at most, a two-month suspensive veto.

Prime Minister Trudeau sought to maximize support for his proposals. Various provincial premiers and provincial pressure groups – with no electoral mandate for their ideas – favoured provincial power to appoint the members of a house that would become, by definition, a 'House of the Provinces.' Prime Minister Trudeau's proposals look like a political compromise. An indirect election system was a *via media* between a purely provincial, patronage-ridden appointment system and the modern democratic principle of direct, popular election. It fails to meet the test of a genuine constitutional reform, and should be modified accordingly to provide for direct popular election on a proportional representation basis within province-wide boundaries.

In general, the federal government's proposal for a new 'House of the Federation' seems to have been intended and designed as a political compromise. Its aim was to blunt some of the current drives by various intransigent English-speaking premiers not so much to reform or restructure the existing Senate as to substitute for it a wholly different type of institution, a 'House of the Provinces,' which would be the creature of, and solely responsible to, the provincial governments.

11
Sober Second Thoughts

The Special Joint Committee of the Senate and of the House of Commons on the Constitution of Canada was set up at the end of June 1978, immediately after Prime Minister Trudeau's release of the text of his Constitutional Amendment Bill, 1978. The committee was to be the first stage of the federal government's plan to revise the constitution, as unfolded in the earlier document, *A Time for Action: Toward the Renewal of the Canadian Federation*.

In the subsequent document accompanying the Constitutional Amendment Bill – the so-called *Highlights* – Prime Minister Trudeau indicated that it was not intended to pass the bill at the then current session of Parliament, but to refer the bill to a joint committee of the Commons and Senate. The government itself would also have intensive discussions with the provinces, including a First Ministers' conference in the fall of 1978. The bill was to 'serve as a basis for public, parliamentary, and inter-governmental discussion,' and was accordingly not presented in final form but was open to amendment.

The committee members, at their first organizational meeting, indicated that they shared the Prime Minister's conception of the bill as a draft. Both the Liberal co-chairman, Mark MacGuigan, and the leading Conservative MP, Flora MacDonald, stated their intention to go beyond the government's constitutional package in the committee's recommendations and indeed to study the general subject of constitutional reform.

MacGuigan had also been co-chairman of the Molgat-MacGuigan Committee. His co-chairman now was Senator Maurice Lamontagne. Composed of 20 MPs and 15 senators, the committee included many experienced people: Robert Stanfield, former Leader of the Opposition; Ed Broadbent, Leader of the New Democratic Party; three former provincial premiers – Duff Roblin of Manitoba, and Henry Hicks and George Smith of Nova Scotia (all senators);

Senator Eugene Forsey; and Senator Molgat, co-chairman of the Molgat-MacGuigan Committee.

The committee began its hearings on 15 August 1978, with plans to hear members of the federal and provincial governments, representatives of private pressure groups and interest associations, and constitutional specialists. Unfortunately, it had only a skeleton staff and no general counsel, and was required to present a report to Parliament when it re-convened on 10 October. This deadline necessitated working through the late summer and effectively prevented any hearings outside Ottawa or any long-range research.

A somewhat ambiguous element in the committee's work was the rôle of the senators. The Senate had established its own Special Committee on the Constitution which began work on 8 August and operated more or less in tandem with the Joint Committee by conducting its own hearings with specialist witnesses. In truth, the Senate committee was effectively pre-empted by the Joint Committee with its wider range of concern. The Senate committee nevertheless did some important work.

Its *First Report*,[1] officially submitted by the chairman, Senator Richard J. Stanbury, on 19 October 1978, contained the implicit hope of a further extension of life in the future. However, the Senate committee heard only ten witnesses: three senior federal civil servants, and two provincial functionaries from British Columbia pleading the already lost cause of a *Bundesrat*-style Senate; the remaining five witnesses included J.C. McRuer, the distinguished former Chief Justice of the High Court of Ontario and specialist in administrative law reform, and four academics. None of these had, so far as is known, previously written on the Senate or on the rôle of federal upper houses or the legislative processes generally. The Senate committee did not, however, limit itself, in its seventeen-page report, to Senate questions. Instead, it ranged very widely over the whole of Bill C-60, with comments, in passing, upon the 'drafting style' of the federal bill: 'The drafting ... leaves very much to be desired in many cases'; 'elephantine sections with numerous subsections and paragraphs'; 'someone has said the Bill reads like a lease, others have said that it reads like the Income Tax Act.'

The Senate committee observed that 'some of the fears expressed on the subject of the provisions relating to the monarchy, the Governor General and the cabinet have exaggerated the extent of the changes proposed in the Bill.' It also expressed the need for 'the utmost caution' with respect to the 'attempt to put the conventions, customs and usages of the Constitution into a text of law.'

On the Supreme Court of Canada, the committee considered that membership should remain at nine judges because any increase would make for more judicial opinions and hence for more difficulty in finding the *ratio deci-dendi* in any case. One may agree with the conclusion, but not necessarily with the reasoning. An increase in membership from nine to eleven judges as Bill C-60 proposed would no doubt make for a small increase in the number of judicial opinions in any case. It could hardly affect the principal difficulty in finding any clear *ratio decidendi* in Canadian Supreme Court decisions. This lies in the relative absence, in comparison to final appellate tribunals in other countries, of internal court organization to produce a common opinion of the court, representing an agreed, lowest common denominator of majority thinking in any case.

The Senate committee rejected the idea in Bill C-60 of ratification of nominations to the Supreme Court by the federal upper house. It favoured a more informal process of federal government consultation with the provinces prior to any such nomination of judges. The committee indicated its doubts as to the wisdom or utility of confining Quebec civil law questions to the Quebec judges on the court, expressing its view that 'the problem being addressed is more "felt" or perceived, than real.' The committee concluded that there was no evidence that 'the participation of common law judges in civil law cases was doing violence to civil law jurisprudence.' Two short and succinct tables on actual voting in the Supreme Court on Quebec civil law questions, 1960 to 1966, and 1967 to 1978, were appended to the report. They seem amply to confirm the committee's conclusion and to dispel an old myth once and for all.

It was on the Senate itself, however, that the recommendations of the committee were most eagerly awaited. Quite predictably, the report essentially favoured the *status quo*. It rejected the idea of an elected Senate: 'One must be realistic, however; the House of Commons would not tolerate such a change.' It also rejected the Bill C-60 'House of the Federation,' with its proposed mix of 'federal' and 'provincial' senators. By implication, though not in terms, it rejected demands for a wholly provincially appointed 'House of the Provinces' in place of the Senate. The committee also 'detects an underlying confusion in the minds of the proponents of Bill C-60 between a federal-provincial conclave and a parliamentary second chamber.' This well-justified rebuke could be more appropriately directed to the more intransigent provincial proponents of a 'House of the Provinces' than to Prime Minister Trudeau. He, after all, simply bought half of a bad idea and tried to modernize and democratize it by substituting election – albeit indirect – for the purely patronage appointments system favoured by its original sponsors.

On the whole, the 'Senate' sections of the report are too skimpy and too lacking in supporting citations and argumenation to be intellectually very persuasive. This is quite apart from the charge of political special pleading that attaches too easily to the committee's recommendation against any substantial restructuring or even abolition of the Senate itself. The report contains interesting appraisals and aperçus, but needs far more sustained research and argumentation to command authority.

In contrast, the Joint Committee laboured throughout the later summer months, heard almost fifty witnesses, and received written submissions from a further few hundred. Yet its report, presented to Parliament on 10 October 1978, was more consciously restrained and concentrated in its discussions and recommendations. It is styled an 'Interim Report.'[2] The committee would have to be formally 'continued' if it were to survive in the session of Parliament after 10 October, and the government might take advantage of the opportunity of reconstituting the committee, possibly without the Senate members, in view of the Senate's own committee. The task of assessing and appraising recommendations for constitutional change was big enough, however, in the committee's opinion, to warrant a further, final report. They were also awaiting the 1978 First Ministers' constitutional conference and the submission of the report of the Pépin-Robarts Commission (see pages 155-6).

The report noted, at the outset, the controversy over the *process* of constitutional change and in particular over the federal government's power to act of its own accord in terms of the BNA Act (No. 2) 1949. No consensus emerged among the expert constitutional witnesses appearing before the committee as to this point. The committee had adopted a resolution (by a vote of nineteen to eleven), recommending that the federal government refer to the Supreme Court for advisory opinion on the constitutionality or otherwise of acting alone in respect to the Senate and the position of the Crown. In September 1978, the federal Minister of Justice agreed to seek an advisory opinion from the Supreme Court with regard to the Senate, but declined to refer those sections dealing with the Crown and the office of Governor-General on the ground that no change of the constitutional rôle or powers of these two offices was intended. The reference to the Supreme Court concerning the Senate was formally made in late November 1978.

The provinces had objected, particularly in the Regina communiqué of 10 August 1978, to the federal government's separating federal institutional change from division of powers questions. The committee felt that the Prime Minister's announced willingness to discuss these questions at the First Ministers' constitutional conference should help ease its future work.

The committee recommended more conscious inspiration and conciseness in style and content in the Preamble and Statement of Aims of Canadian Federation in Bill C-60. It favoured an entrenched constitutional Charter of Rights and Freedoms, and also supported 'meaningful constitutional guarantees for the use of English and French and in the field of education.' It affirmed the 'need to protect basic linguistic rights by means of constitutional guarantees,' though stating, at the same time, that 'Ultimately, the progress of bilingualism in Canada will depend upon the evolution of public opinion, not on compulsion.'

As to institutions, the committee had no specific recommendations to make. It simply recorded differences of opinion, within the committee itself, as to whether the bill as drafted did or did not significantly change the rôle of the monarchy in Canada. It noted the Prime Minister's statement that the bill simply stated the 'present reality as it is, taking into account the developments in our constitutional practice since 1867.' The Special Committee pointed out, here, that 'A number of Members of the Committee think it undesirable to codify the functions of all the major institutions of government which are now defined largely by evolving conventions.'

As for the Supreme Court, the committee could only agree to record the expressions of concern by witnesses about the method of appointment of judges to the Supreme Court proposed in Bill C-60, and about various provincial proposals for 'providing regional representations' on the court.

Finally, the committee commented upon the very wide range of opinion, offered in testimony before it, as to the Senate. Four main models had been presented – a popularly elected Senate; Bill C-60's House of the Federation; a West German *Bundesrat*-style 'House of the Provinces'; and modified versions of the existing Senate. There was simply no agreement among witnesses. The committee did not, in consequence, feel able to make any specific recommendations on the Senate, though it did go on record that 'the overwhelming body of witnesses and a substantial majority of the members of the Committee are prepared to recommend ... that the Parliament of Canada should have a second Chamber and that the Senate as now constituted should be reformed.'

After so much concentrated hard work on the part of members, and the extent and depth of their cross-examination of expert witnesses, such a meagre consensus may seem rather disappointing. It was limited essentially to the recommendation of a redrafting of the statement of aims in the preamble to Bill C-60, with a view to conciseness, style, and language, and to the adoption of an entrenched constitutional charter of rights and freedoms. The committee had decided upon the principle of a unanimous interim report. It was more or less inevitable that it would end up either with a bland or ambiguous report, or – as it in fact did – with a reasonably succinct and tightly written report limited to those few matters upon which a genuine, all-party consensus was possible. The usual differences of opinion in a report accompanied by dissenting opinions would have to await a final report. The committee itself recommended that it should be 'continued' in the new session of Parliament and be provided with expert assistance and staffing.

The Bar Association Special Committee on the Constitution (see pages 120–1) stands as an example that intelligence, allied with enthusiasm, is not enough to achieve a breakthrough in the current Canadian constitutional dialogue. The special committee perhaps started off on the wrong foot. Its members were not elected but were directly appointed under the prerogative powers of the president of the association. Of the twelve members of the special committee only two seem to have had contact, in professional legal practice, with constitutional law cases. This might not have affected the claims of the final report as a representative bar opinion, if the committee had sampled or polled rank-and-file bar attitudes on the constitution in general and on constitutional change in particular. This the committee did not do, perhaps because it thought the time – twelve months – was too short, even with a $250,000 budget to draw upon.

When the report was finally published in August 1978, it was shown to be out of touch with rank-and-file opinion in its recommendation that the Queen be replaced by a new titular head of state elected by the lower house of Parliament. This was the rock on which the whole report and all its detailed recommendations on the whole gamut of constitutional matters sundered. The rank-and-file members of the bar, at the 1978 Annual General Meeting, voted in effect to consign the report to limbo.

If the report be thought of, however, not as a 'representative' bar opinion, but as a venture in academic legal research in its own right, then certain further reservations must be advanced; this despite the fact that the special committee was able to engage the services of a highly qualified research director.

Perhaps because of time constraints, the report has no foot-noting, no documentation, and no appendices. Its recommendations emerge as *ex cathedra* utterances, resting on the word of the committee itself. There is very little evidence of a sustained attempt on the part of the members to fill the gaps in their own constitutional knowledge by organized consultation with constitutional specialists, either comparative or Canadian. Such outside expert advice as there was, while undoubtedly highly qualified, was spasmodic, unsystematic, and limited in the range and coverage of the matters examined.

The report also omits the nuances and qualifications – in otherwise too categorical recommendations – that would be provided by publication of dissenting opinions within its own ranks. In the end, apart from the disastrous recommendation as to the head of state, the report says little that is new. It limits itself essentially to reiterating constitutional projects already advanced by various political pressure groups or special interest associations, including that of replacing the Senate by a *Bundesrat*.

The '*Bundesrat* caper' emerged innocently enough, in late 1977, in the discovery by BC Premier Bennett that the *Bundesrat* is the apogée of contemporary constitutionalism. It had been imposed on Germany by the American Military Government in 1949 to educate the West Germans in democracy. Premier Bennett's constitutional revelation was followed by a flying 'Cook's Tour' to West Germany in January 1978 by his Minister for Consumer Affairs. The minister returned extolling the virtues of the *Bundesrat*; and so, *qua* institution, it immediately entered the BC government's constitutional package for recasting of the Canadian federal system.

Within the space of a few months, by the spring of 1978, it had been officially embraced by such diverse groups as Premier Davis' Advisory Committee on Confederation, the federal Progressive Conservative party, and the Canada West Foundation (a private foundation financed, in considerable part, by the four western provinces' governments).[3] In August 1978 it turned up again as a recommendation in the ill-fated report of the Committee on the Constitution of the Canadian Bar Association.

It is perhaps a commentary on comparative constitutional law research in Canada and on the interlocking character of the various political parties and public and private pressure groups on the constitution that such a casually developed and badly researched idea as the *Bundesrat* should go so far, so quickly. For it is an ill-researched idea! The Bonn Constitution as a whole was not imposed by the Americans on Germany after 1945. Such an interpretation ignores the very positive rôle of Konrad Adenauer and the leaders of all the main political parties in the actual constitution-making.

The *Bundesrat* was not a new institution invented by the Western Allies for the contingencies of occupation. It had substantial antecedents in the Bismarckian federal constitutional system of 1871, and its ultimate roots lie in German constitutional history in the earlier princely conclaves of the Holy Roman Empire.

Beyond that, the *Bundesrat* is not even a federal upper house or an autonomous legislative body – so the West German *Bundesverfassungsgericht* (special constitutional court) has ruled. It is limited to cooperating with the *Bundestag* (federal legislative assembly) on legislation.

Those provincial politicians and others who have combined to sponsor a *Bundesrat*-style 'House of the Provinces' are indulging in a confusion (apparently an unwitting one), between *executive* and *legislative* power. For, in its historical origins and in its latter-day practice under the Bonn Constitution of 1949, the *Bundesrat* more nearly resembles the Canadian First Ministers' conferences than a *bona fide* legislative chamber. We have our own distinctive Canadian institution – the First Ministers' conference – that is capable of further organic growth in its own right. Should we not try to build on, develop, and strengthen that institution? Is that not wiser than to try to convert an existing federal *legislative* institution, the Senate, into one's own mistaken image of a foreign federal executive institution? After all, the general attrition of the *legislative* process – in Canada not less than in other western countries – is a key factor in the general constitutional *malaise* of post-industrial society. The Canada West Foundation was one of the groups originally sponsoring a *Bundesrat*-style conclave in replacement of the existing federal Senate. To its credit, and after reflection, the foundation seems finally to have abandoned the idea, as can be seen in its testimony before the Senate-House Special Joint Committee on the Constitution.[4]

In the Canadian constitutional debate since the November 1976 Quebec election, the English-speaking provinces have generally been seizing the initiative in constitutional changes. The Quebec government is officially committed to separatism and not to change within Confederation, and is silent on this point.

Most of the English-speaking constitutional claims are officially advanced to meet Quebec's demands. They seem on examination, however, to have very little indeed to do with Quebec's special claims but to amount instead to constitutional special pleadings designed to meet the special interests of the premiers concerned. They desire to participate more directly in federal government decision-making or federal government patronage, in the name of a general decentralization. These constitutional complaints would be more persuasive if they could claim general popular support. But so far no premier outside Quebec has obtained an electoral mandate in favour of constitutional decentralization or constitutional change in general. These particular complaints would also be more impressive intellectually if they could demonstrate academic and professional legal backing over a period of years comparable to the sustained support accorded by Quebec's intellectual establishment to Quebec's special constitutional demands.

In the absence of both these elements the English-speaking premiers' claims remain, at best, political debating points or expendable negotiating positions, in no way corresponding in political authority to the constitutional claims of successive Quebec governments since 1960. They have, in any case, nothing to do with the '*deux nations*' approach to Canadian federalism.

They are only interesting, from the viewpoint of legal theory, because of their as yet surprisingly uncontested pretension to displace the federal government and the MPs as constitutional spokesmen for the people of those provinces. There is little in all this to displace the broad conclusion that, beside the future of Quebec itself, the key new issues in any constitutional change for Canada will be 'general,' non-federal issues. Perhaps most significant is the redefinition of relations of man and the state. Questions of reform and modernization have already been adverted to by Guy Saint-Pierre and his Quebec cabinet sub-committee. These must include examination of a possible new constitutional rôle and a new and independent tax base for the great metropolitan urban concentrations like Toronto, Montreal and Vancouver. The process of continuing, incremental constitutional change, in operation since the adoption of the BNA Act of 1867, will undoubtedly have to respond to these matters – in addition to its necessary attention to specifically 'Quebec' questions – in the very near future.

12
No Easy Answers

Frank Scott noted that he used to tell his law students: 'We have a *rendez-vous* with the BNA Act. It's going to come some day!' The BNA Act is likely to be around for some considerable time longer. It hasn't worked too badly by the test of time; and there just isn't enough consensus on the need for change and the means and the directions of that change, for us to believe that outright rewriting of the constitution can proceed with any reasonable prospects of success.

Change in the constitution and the constitutional system will occur, as it has occurred continually from 1867 onwards, in response to changes in Canadian society. But it is most likely to be gradual, organic change that builds upon and extends the existing constitutional arrangements, and not a wholesale abolition of the BNA Act and its replacement by something altogether new.

The fault (if fault there has been) in federal-provincial constitutional relations in recent years has not been the division of powers as such, but the people who have been authoritatively interpreting and applying it. A constitution is not a municipal ordinance on sewers and drains that can or needs to be drafted precisely and rigidly to avoid any room for interpretation and discussion in the future. Being intended to stand for some time, a constitutional charter will normally be formulated at a certain level of generality and abstraction, to facilitate its creative adjustment to changing conditions and new demands not always anticipated by its original drafters. This certainly has happened to the BNA Act over the years and explains the pendulum-like swings in its rôle as constitutional 'law-in-action.' It could, of course, as easily change again and yield to current centrifugal pressures, without any change at all in the letter of the sections 91 and 92 division of legislative competence; and there are already good signs of just such a new, pluralist emphasis in Canadian federalism for the future, in response to Quebec's questioning of the *status quo*. It would be possible of course, as an abstract exercise in legal drafting, to make sections 91 and 92 of the BNA Act appear relatively fool-proof, by rendering them so precise and detailed as to exclude any possible equivocation. Even, however, assuming that the necessary prior political consensus could be obtained on undertaking this exercise and reaching timely agreement on the new contents of sections 91 and 92, they would likely become out-dated from the moment of their adoption, as entirely new problems emerge in a rapidly evolving society. The quest for an elaborate constitutional blueprint to cover all future problems of society is likely to be quite illusory, as comparative constitutional law shows. It would seem much more fruitful, if change is desired, to change the legal 'honoratiores' who will be authoritatively interpreting and applying them – the Supreme Court judges, for example.

The Constitutional Amendment Bill, 1978, in fact provides just such an opening, with its suggestions for modest changes in the structure of the court and the method of nomination and appointment of its judges. Even here, however, it may be less a matter of changing the judges than of changing their methods of interpretation and their philosophy of judicial review. Courts do, in fact, read the election returns – as was alleged before, during, and after the 1937 US 'Court Revolution.' It has been a truism of comparative constitutional law that Supreme Court majorities have rarely remained too long out of step with overall governmental and community trends.

It is therefore perhaps surprising that so well respected a student of constitutional law and government as Claude Ryan, in his first criticisms of the Constitutional Amendment Bill, 1978, should appear to opt for a thorough-going approach to constitutional change. He criticized the proposals for failing to tackle both federal institutional change and constitutional division of powers at the same time.[1] The record of the last several years, in any case, suggests more federal governmental sensitivity to the all too frequent complaint from Quebec and other provinces that the Supreme Court is just another instrument of federal government power. More governmental attention to, and public discussion of, the philosophy of a candidate for judicial office may not be necessary. However, we should certainly see more conscious federal executive self-restraint in the referring of constitutional conflicts with the provinces to the courts, and in the intervening in constitutional litigation involving the provinces. We may also see more judicial self-restraint in extending constitutional jurisdiction in cases where private pressure groups or associations or individuals seek to impugn provincial legislative action by invoking the federal constitutional issue.

A selective approach to constitutional change does not of course exclude eventual overall change. It does involve the establishment of the priority issues and their ranking in some sort of hierarchy for problem-solving purposes, which may mean identifying their intrinsic importance and quantifying their social costs – including relative degree of community resistance to change in a particular area or areas. Intellectual resistance has often surfaced on the part of English-speaking, common-law-trained constitutionalists and political leaders to abstract *a priori* categories postulated in advance of concrete problems. Such concepts as '*deux nations*,' 'associate state,' 'special' or 'particular' constitutional status, or, latterly, '*souveraineté-association*,' have created in advance formidable psychological barriers to the discussion of any form of constitutional change.

Public attitudes can of course change by dint of simple repetition. They can also change through a more sophisticated awareness on the part of both French-Canadian civil lawyers and English-Canadian common lawyers of the distinctive legal philosophy and methodology of the two systems that co-exist within Canadian jurisprudence. Civil lawyers tend to start with an abstract conception or legal definition, and then refine or adapt it to political exigencies as these emerge in concrete situations. Common lawyers eschew abstract general categories except as they emerge inductively from specific low-level problems and their low-level solutions.

Conceptions like 'special,' 'particular,' or 'associate state' status may have appeared appropriate to Quebec spokesmen in the 1960s as rallying points for changing the federal system. But they aroused instinctive opposition from their English-speaking counterparts even without any examination of their detailed, low-level, substantive legal implications for Canadian federalism. Discussion of the latter might have revealed points of common interest and concern on constitutional change and facilitated the building of political bridges between the two legal systems. The notion of special status for Quebec – but not necessarily for the other provinces – would not have developed into the *bête noire* that it became for English Canada. This reaction created a psychological barrier to the idea of any constitutional change in response to Quebec's dilemma.

Public attitudes can change in time, involving both the voters and their leaders. John Robarts was noted for his open attitude, all too rare at the time, towards French Canada. He remarked recently that the intellectual climate had changed sufficiently for one to be able now to discuss, in English-speaking legal circles, the idea of a special constitutional status for Quebec without arousing an immediate angry reaction and refusal to speak further. For many English-speaking lawyers, indeed, special constitutional status for Quebec offers immediate political advantages. It avoids any need for cataclysmic changes in the constitutional system – involving *all* the English-speaking provinces equally with Quebec – which might become immediately outdated if Quebec should leave. Such changes would, in any case, create the great risk of an unworkable federal system in which key economic decision-making powers had been decentralized away to vanishing point.

Special constitutional status – no longer seen as a single, comprehensive package of non-negotiable constitutional demands – also lends itself very easily to the pragmatic approach to constitutional change. That is in fact the way Ottawa and Quebec, very quietly but nevertheless unmistakably, have been proceeding since November 1976. They have been trying to reach practical accommodations in areas such as immigration and cable television where political good sense and good public administration suggest joint, cooperative, federal-provincial decision-making.

A further merit of this approach is that it need not remain so very 'special,' in the sense of being unique or exclusive to Ottawa-Quebec relations. One English-speaking premier wondered aloud why Quebec should be given a special deal on participation in decision-making on immigration matters. He was reminded that it would only remain 'special' (limited to Quebec) so long as his own and other provinces did not find it helpful or useful to ask Ottawa for similar special arrangements for their own provinces.

There was nothing in the new conception of *ad hoc* special constitutional status preventing provinces other than Quebec from making similar arrangements if both they and the federal government should want to reach agreement thereon. There is nothing in the history and practice of federalism preventing any such special arrangements for one or more provinces according to their special conditions or needs. Such arrangements and the pragmatic accommodations and adjustments that they involve are essential to a working federal system.

Equally as impressive as the changes in basic English-Canadian attitudes towards the idea of special constitutional status for Quebec are the changes in attitudes towards the 'French fact' in Quebec.

The federal government has resisted all the temptations to launch a guerrilla war of litigation against Quebec's Bill 22 and Bill 101. There has, in addition, been no significant public demand, outside Quebec, for any such intervention against the Quebec government.

The primacy of the 'French fact' in Quebec and the notion that Quebec will become as French as the other provinces are English[2] are being determined by the survival and implementation of Quebec's language legislation and its *de facto* acceptance within Quebec itself. English-speaking communities there are either acquiescing in the spirit and the letter of the legislation, or applying the remedy available within a federal country of moving to other provinces.[3] In any case, the 'Frenchness' of Quebec – in the social as well as strictly linguistic implications of the two Quebec bills – is being consummated right now. It can hardly be reversed, whatever changes of regime may occur in the immediate future.

What is to be the policy of a resolutely 'French' Quebec towards its own non-francophone minorities? Both Quebec language bills accord significant *de jure* protection to the anglophone minorities, though there may be argument on the relative tactfulness, politeness, or generosity with which each approaches that problem. Clearly, however, the new, pluralistic approach to federalism indicates that such protection of minority linguistic interests can most effectively be applied at the provincial and not at the federal government level. For the federal government to intervene, sword in hand, is to invite resistance and failure at the 'living-law' level of community attitudes and practices. 'Truth,' as the great Protestant theologian, Reinhold Niebuhr, observed, 'often marches into history on the back of an error.' The trial-and-error testing and experimentation inherent in federalism suggest that the practical effectuation of protection of minority language interests is best left to provincial governments, in the first instance at least.

English-Canadian attitudes to civil liberties in Quebec are largely determined by the great 1950s constitutional battles launched before the Supreme Court of Canada by the Jehovah's Witnesses against the Duplessis government and the Catholic hierarchy of Quebec. It is difficult to shift a dominant English-Canadian image based on triumphant 'Anglo-Saxon' judicial majorities within the Supreme Court of Canada successfully imposing 'open society' civil libertarian values upon French-Canadian judicial minorities.

Such simplistic conclusions from past history tend to ignore how much Quebec society has changed, and the dramatic changes in Quebec executive, legislative, and judicial attitudes since that time. There have been liberal legislative innovations like the Bill of Rights annexed to the new Quebec Civil Code, and the inspired and magnanimous court judgments rendered by Chief Judge Deschênes. All this suggests it would be wise to avoid federal government and federal court paternalism and imposed federal solutions for peculiarly Quebec problems. These matters should be left to the operation of the ordinary political processes within Quebec and to ordinary litigation before Quebec courts.

If Quebec is becoming as 'French' as the other provinces are 'English,' what does that do to national language policy? Whither the federal Official Languages Act of 1969 and incipient federal government attitudes towards what is now called multiculturalism? The Official Languages Act was posited upon a 'personal' rather than a 'territorial' notion of the desirable Canadian national language policy. Every Canadian citizen, whether francophone or anglophone in origin, was to be able to use and be served in his maternal language anywhere in Canada.

While the federal act was, of necessity, limited to areas of federal legislative competence under the BNA Act, it had more general philosophic implications. It rejected the notion of 'territoriality' of language. The territorial approach meant responding to the sociological facts of the existing linguistic distribution within Canada and recognizing that, while Quebec was undoubtedly French with only a small, vestigial English-language minority, the other provinces (with the possible exception of New Brunswick) were irretrievably English. The territorial approach, applied by provincial governments within such areas of provincial competence as culture and education, meant that Canadian citizens leaving their original home province to reside in another province must accept that province's language. They did not carry with them, so to speak, their own special body of 'personal' law, including a right to demand and receive provincial government services in their own language.

There is little doubt that, after nearly a decade of experience and application of the official language program, those policies have failed to implement bilingualism nationally in federal government services and, by way of moral persuasion or example, in provincial government administrative and educational services.[4] The Official Languages Commissioner, Keith Spicer, points in his annual reports to obvious errors of overly enthusiastic, even Draconian, application of the bilingual program by federal administrators in ways that were surely counter-productive. But the real constraints were surely objective factors of geography, distance, and the movement of trade, goods, and services.

What seems to be emerging is a more modest and humane federal bilingual program limited to federal services and with a large element of pragmatism in its practical application. This accompanies or, more properly, co-exists with provincial language programs. These are determinedly territorial in their philosophy and also, by and large, unilingual in scope, save only for some deference to the language interests of any existing second-official-language minority within the territorial frontiers of the province. This means in Quebec official acceptance, despite the proclamation of French as the official language of Quebec, of a legal right to be educated in English on the part of persons born within the province whose *bona fide* maternal language is English. It means, in other provinces, some very modest and limited provisions for education in French under certain specified circumstances.

The trend in all provinces today, paralleling the acceptance of the territorially based, unilingual approach, seems to be to augment the facilities offered in the second official language. This, coupled with the modified federal bilingual program and some increased federal assistance to cultural groups outside the two official language groups, is in line with the new pluralism in Canadian constitutional law. In its acceptance of two territorially based, *de facto* separate and distinct language units, this solution has elements in common with Belgian arrangements. However it is something more than a 'Belgian' solution in the hope it offers that both language communities will render justice to the minorities of the other language group and accord them privileged language status within each province.

To recapitulate one of our opening points, most of the problems of contemporary federal systems, including Canada's, are not constitutional but societal, and a constitutional charter will have at best only a marginal effect on those problems.

The crises of contemporary federal systems may not be intrinsically different from those affecting other, post-industrial societies that have, by contrast, a unitary governmental system. There is the problem of the coexistence at the same time of high inflation and high unemployment; the conflict between the exigencies of large-scale industrialization and demands for protection of life-style and the environment; the manifest and increasing alienation of large sections of the population who feel excluded from the rewards of the consumer society.

Most democratic systems today have little to say on these problems and offer only a civilized, orderly process whereby a new consensus on the distribution and allocation of goods and services can perhaps be translated into legislative form. This does not always occur without unnecessary delays or institutional encumbrances. Long gone are the days when democratic constitutionalism, in the name of 'due process' or some equivalent verbal formula, could succeed in maintaining a socio-economic philosophy such as political *laissez-faire* in the face of the general winds of change in the community. Those days ended, once and for all, with Franklin Roosevelt's re-election victory in 1936 and the resultant capitulation of the conservative majority on the Supreme Court.

Democratic constitutionalism today is determinedly impartial in social and economic terms, and the Canadian constitution – the BNA Act of 1867 – has the advantage of being completely neutral, in ideological terms, in its main verbal formulations. The BNA Act imposed no obstacle to changing majorities in Parliament or in provincial houses seeking to implement special economic mandates. The Bennett 'New Deal' was already a political dead letter when Mackenzie King referred it to the courts for its constitutional *quietus*. In Alberta, the Aberhart Social Credit government banking and public finance package of the late 1930s contained too many patent errors from the purely technical legal viewpoint.

Even today, except for the very limited stipulations contained in section 133 on the use of French and English in the Quebec legislature and in Quebec courts, the BNA Act imposes no necessary or inevitable barrier to the legislative realization and consummation of the 'French fact' in Quebec. It does not affect the social and economic revolution or the transfer of economic decision-making power implicit in Bill 22 and Bill 101.

One may pose the real constitutional dilemma in the following way. The existing federal constitution has not obstructed the translation of Quebec's Quiet Revolution into institutional form. Is it really necessary for English Canada to undertake major constitutional projects on the basis that they are necessary to keep Quebec within Confederation? If the existing federal constitution is not the real problem, must Quebec leave Confederation or otherwise attenuate it through separation, '*souveraineté-association*,' or similar new constitutional formulae?

There will be, at intervals in a country's history, times that are ripe for acts of legal codification, and other times – much more common – that are hardly propitious for any such ventures. In the latter times it is very difficult to produce a charter that will become 'law-in-action.'

The prerequisite for achievement of a successful charter is the existence of a prior societal consensus on the fundamental goals and purposes of the new charter. Even in the comparatively noncontroversial area of codification of the private (civil) law, the German jurist, von Savigny, warned against the dangers of a 'premature' venture in national law-making, before a sufficient national identity had emerged. Hasty action could result in a legal document that would act as a brake on national development and also become instantly out-of-date.

So much more is this true in the case of a constitutional charter: the historical examples drawn from comparative legal science tend to demonstrate that the really successful acts of constitution-making have occurred in periods of public euphoria, often after some great military victory or revolution when a sufficient degree of national consensus as to the basic ends and purposes of society – and also the means and techniques for attaining them – exists, however briefly.

The difficulties with venturing upon the total revision and replacement of the British North America Act of 1867 are self-evident. There are just too many contingencies in the Quebec political situation. It is not wise to make constitutions for what Franklin Roosevelt used to call politically 'iffy' situations; nor to treat ventures in constitution-making as what Justice Owen Roberts of the US Supreme Court, in another context, described as railway excursion tickets good for one journey only on a particular day and to a particular place.

The political situation in Quebec must stabilize, and a clear political consensus emerge on what constitutional changes – if any – would be needed to complete and effectuate the Quiet Revolution, before the rest of the country can act. Replacement or fundamental alteration of the existing federal system, on the notion – essentially of English-speaking leaders – that this is really 'what Quebec wants,' seems misguided. When constitutional changes are advanced by English-speaking leaders, we must be sure that they are changes that are useful and sensible in their own right, whatever Quebec may finally choose to do. They must leave a workable federal system for the rest of the country should Quebec indeed separate from Canada. Some recent constitutional proposals from English-speaking leaders look to be directed more to advancing the parochial special interests of their clients than to finding solutions to the Quebec problem as such.

Constitution-making may have become English Canada's favourite party game, but it remains, nevertheless, a legal exercise, and there are some clear lessons to be drawn from comparative constitutional law as to the traps and pitfalls to be avoided by those who wish to practise it – what we might call the axioms of constitution-making.

There is the story, which is only partly apocryphal, of the pundit who boasted to a social gathering that he was the author of the constitution of a recently independent Commonwealth country until he was introduced to another pundit making exactly the same claim. In fact, the first pundit was the author of the country's *fourth* constitution which had lasted, as I recollect, forty-eight hours; the other wrote the fifth constitution, and it had been stillborn. The country, when the two men met, was into its sixth or seventh charter and still under a military dictatorship. The same point was elegantly made by the authors of the Weimar Constitution of 1919. They confessed to having drafted a model liberal-democratic constitutional charter but to having, now, to find a people worthy of living under it.

The *first* axiom of constitution-making must, therefore, be one of constitutional modesty. The best constitution is one that bears a close relationship to the societal conditions in which it must operate, even if it may not be particularly elegant in its literary formulation or drafting. This is a point to bear in mind when the BNA Act of 1867 is under attack from all sides: poetic it certainly is not, but it does seem to work reasonably well, whereas the 'Sermon on the Mount,' still to be reduced to Canadian constitutional form, may not. This is not so much a case against change in the BNA Act as a case for weighing the case for change soberly, and not rhetorically – and weighing it in the light of particular situations. It may happen that incremental change, through formal revision in specific places or through developing custom and convention, is the remedy, rather than starting again, afresh.

A *second* axiom of contemporary constitution-making is the non-trans-ferability of constitutional institutions from one country to another. Unless the societal conditions under which a particular institution originated and was developed in one country can be reproduced in another country, experi-ments in constitutional eclecticism are likely to be, at best, wildly unpredict-able, and, too often, completely disillusioning.

It is often believed that the West German *Bundesverfassungsgericht*, which was the most interesting and most noble instrument in the revival of demo-cratic constitutionalism in Germany, was borrowed directly from the US Supreme Court. Certainly there was a strong intellectual and moral influence from the United States and from common-law constitutionalism in general in the early years of the Bonn Constitution. But several of the key judges on the West German court had direct, first-hand experience in 'Anglo-Saxon' constitutionalism, and the court itself was firmly rooted in German judicial practice in public-law matters in the Weimar Republic.

The case is not so much against eclecticism, as such, but for recognizing its limitations and for avoiding the search for simplistic solutions from other countries. Normally, the analogy from foreign law is best conceived as a paradigm, whose exact translation from another country to one's own can only be effected under ideal, laboratory conditions.

A *third* axiom, which is almost a subaxiom of the preceding one, is to avoid giving a spurious specificity in constitutional prescriptions. Some of the balloons floated by English-speaking pundits in the current Canadian constitutional debate display just such a vice, apparently being formulated on the principle that if presented categorically they would convey more political conviction. It is better to formulate general guide-lines in advance of actual constitution-making and leave it to the give-and-take and compromise of direct negotiation to produce precise details.

Meanwhile, a pox on those pundits who affirm that they have the answer to Canada's constitutional ills in a new, thirty-man federal upper house or a new eight-man special constitutional court! One wonders if the (non-lawyer) academic authors of the eight-man constitutional court proposals were aware of the problem if the judges divide evenly, and that for this reason it is useful to have an odd number of judges.

A *fourth* axiom concerns the interdependence of constitutional institutions in any system. Change the existing Senate of Canada by increasing its powers *vis-à-vis* the lower house and the Supreme Court, and you automatically change those other institutions in a series of reciprocal causes and effects. Borrow, as some English-speaking leaders have proposed, the West German institution of the *Bundesrat* and install it in Canada, and you wrench it completely out of its West German context unless you also borrow other West German institutions like the *Bundestag* and the *Bundesverfassungsgericht* with which it is inextricably interrelated and interdependent. In a working constitution like Canada's, even piecemeal change needs to be approached carefully, with some estimation of the likely effects, upon other institutions or the constitution as a whole, of altering one institution.

A *fifth* axiom, flowing from the preceding one, is the need to consider the 'digestibility' of any proposals for change. On the whole, one major change to one major institution is about as much as any constitutional system can digest easily at any time. One could change the method of composition of the upper house and its relations to the lower house and the Supreme Court. It might then be prudent and useful to leave these other institutions alone until one can see just what effects the changes in the upper house have on those other institutions and on the constitution as a whole. The argument here is for selectiveness in one's approach to constitutional change. If there is an imbalance in the federal system, choose *either* the upper house *or* something else as a vehicle for constitutional reform, but not all at once.

Thus, several thoughtful English-speaking commentators – J.V. Clyne,[5] and Anthony Westell,[6] for example – have raised the possibility of a change in Canada's federal electoral laws from a first-past-the-post, single-member constituency system to some form of proportional representation on a multi-member constituency, or even province-wide, basis. Such a reform, of and by itself, would probably radically change the Canadian political system. It would no doubt, in producing mixed, multi-party representation from each province, do much to end claims of regional, sectional, or provincial 'alienation' from the federal system as it now exists. But it would seem to be such a big change in itself as to make impossible any simultaneous action on other federal constitutional fronts – the upper house or the Supreme Court.

Should Canadians desire constitutional change – in part, in stages, or all at once and completely – the axioms discussed above may prove useful. But, as mentioned earlier, one would be unwise to expect too much from the mere rewriting of an old constitution or the drafting of a new one.

13
The Continuing Dialectic

The 1978 First Ministers' conference occurred at what *Le Devoir* called 'a strange conjuncture of political events.' It followed substantial losses by the federal Liberal government in the mid-October by-elections; and, in addition, 'public opinion outside Quebec, and for that matter the press which reflected it, waited for nothing more than [Mr Trudeau's] departure and his replacement by another leader.'[1]

Yet, for all that, Prime Minister Trudeau appeared firmly in control of events, both before and during the conference. In his preliminary letter to the provincial premiers, establishing the agenda, he demonstrated flexibility concerning Bill C-60. First, he indicated that there would be no need to give time to those parts of Bill C-60 treating of the monarchy and the titular head of state functions. He cited here the view of 'all the governments' that there was no need for changes in these areas of the constitution. Again, he stated that the federal government attached 'a very great importance' to the division of powers, and would be prepared to have a full exchange of views with the provincial premiers. He thus changed his earlier, June, position that these were 'subsequent' questions, to be dealt with only after the institutional changes proposed in Bill C-60 were adopted.

Most of all, however, Trudeau and the federal government were helped by the absence of a single, unified provincial position on constitutional change. Far from there being any 'ganging up' of provincial premiers in a common front against the federal government, it was revealed quite clearly that there were different attitudes on different subjects, based upon the various provinces' basic interests, resources, and needs. Even the much heralded 'Western unity' turned out to be a myth, collapsing altogether when the time came to descend from abstract constitutional rhetoric to concrete constitutional particulars.[2]

Within the conference, some delegations were clearly more influential than others. Apart from the federal government, these included Ontario, because of its industrial base, its population, and its dominant rôle in Confederation since 1867; and Quebec, because its future remains the central enigma in Canadian constitutional law today. (The Quebec government had finally decided to take part in the conference.)[3] Also important were Alberta, because of its vast natural resources and the strong personality of its premier, and Saskatchewan, not so much perhaps because of its natural resources but because of the intellectual qualities of its premier. With Ontario and Quebec they made up a group of powerful provincial delegations able to bargain with the federal government on something approaching equal terms – intellectually, if not politically.

But the divergence in provincial positions served, if anything, as a vindication of the federal system in Canada. For the four Atlantic 'have-not' provinces, a strong federal government remained necessary to redress the economic imbalance existing, now as before, between the rest of Canada and themselves. They showed no interest at all in proposals from far wealthier provinces for carving up federal competences or for weakening the main federal institutions in the name of constitutional 'reform.'

As for the other provinces, there was absolutely no consensus as to the direction and degree of federal institutional change. British Columbia's premier, predictably enough, found no support for his new, five-region Canadian federation that would up-grade British Columbia but would down-grade the other western provinces and the Atlantic provinces. He also found himself alone with his new 'House of the Provinces' to replace the present Senate. Why should such powerful premiers as Lougheed and Blakeney cede their power to communicate directly with the federal Prime Minister to some new patronage-ridden institutional intermediary?

On the other hand, Prime Minister Trudeau found the provinces did not join with him in giving any particular urgency to the 'patriation' of the constitution. Bringing it to Canada as an act of the Canadian Parliament seemed essentially symbolic or honorific. It would change nothing in terms of the realities of political and economic power in Canada; and was therefore of low priority in comparison to other, more immediate problems. The same might apply to proposals for constitutional amending machinery. It was important to decide on what should be put in any new federal constitutional system, before bothering about how to change it again in the future.

Even the Prime Minister's proposal for an 'entrenched' Bill of Rights, within the BNA Act itself, and for action on language rights, brought no responsive wave of enthusiasm from the provinces. The four western provinces, Ontario, and Quebec seem to have felt that civil rights in Canada were not in danger at the present time. In any case, the statutory Bill of Rights of 1960 has done all that might be necessary on this point. A constitutionally 'entrenched' Bill of Rights would, in any case, open the way to more judicial interpretation and put more provincial laws at the mercy of the current 'pro-Ottawa' Supreme Court.[4] Provincial opinion, here, seemed to vindicate the older, 'received' British constitutional principle of parliamentary supremacy against the newer, 'received' American constitutional principle of the supremacy of the judges.[5]

On the second day of the conference, Trudeau introduced the issue of section 91 and section 92 of the constitution and defined seven substantive matters as open to discussion with a view to a possible new federal-provincial accord. He went to the core of current conflicts within Confederation which had been touched on already, tangentially or indirectly, in his earlier proposals on the restructuring of existing federal institutions.

The seven substantive items were: the federal 'spending' power and its possible limitation in the future; the 'equalisation' system and the federal government's obligations to regional development; the federal declaratory power as to provincial works, and its possible limitation; an authority to the provincial governments to levy indirect taxes (as well as the power of direct taxation which they now have), subject only to the limitation that such provincial indirect taxes must not damage inter-provincial or international commerce; a clarification of the respective powers of the federal and the provincial governments on the regulation, management, and taxation of natural resources, and the administration and regulation in the matter of inter-provincial and international commerce; the unification of family law under provincial jurisdiction; and a recognition in principle that communications constitute one of those areas in which the *two* orders of government, federal and provincial, have legitimate and reasonable interests.

To reach a consensus on a new and more rational allocation of the respective competences would remove the principal tensions of federal-provincial relations of recent years. It would obviate – for now at least – any need for some of the wilder current proposals for reform of existing federal institutions like the Supreme Court and the Senate. These have been advanced by some of the provinces, and already partially accepted by Ottawa as a defensive reaction to intransigent provincial pressures on those institutions.[6]

Indeed, action on only two of the seven items – provincial power to levy indirect taxes and to regulate, manage, and tax natural resources – would meet Alberta and Saskatchewan's complaints against recent Supreme Court decisions. Appropriate action on a third item, communications, would take care of Quebec's major constitutional complaint against Ottawa. This is not to say that the remaining items are not important or that there are not other items in sections 91 and 92 that could be added in the future. It is simply that the three items mentioned are the only ones now involving significant confrontations.

All this seems to confirm the point advanced earlier on the non-necessity of total constitutional rewriting at this time. There should, instead, be limited change directed to specific areas of federal-provincial relations. The various proposals for constitutional reform today are alternative or competing proposals. They differ principally in their modalities or points of contact with the constitutional system as a whole but are addressed to the same problem. They are often different sides of the same coin. Thus the complaints of Alberta and Saskatchewan, and of other provinces too, over recent Supreme Court decisions could be met by changing the court's jurisprudence (case law) or by redefining the specific areas of the constitution (sections 91 and 92) being interpreted.

To change the court's jurisprudence, one can change the judges and the rules of appointment, as FDR tried in 1937. However, the well-known constitutional principle of economy in the use of power would suggest encouraging the court to change its own mind and to retrace the reasoning and philosophical rationale of those particular decisions. Our Supreme Court has undergone cyclical swings in its interpretation of the BNA Act, between favouring the federal government and favouring the provinces. It could perhaps do so again without damaging either its intellectual integrity or its credibility.

The federal government could, of course, help by use of more self-restraint in the reference of, or intervention in, federal-provincial issues before the Supreme Court. Behind this argument lies the assumption that there is nothing inherently wrong with the current division of powers, and that they remain sufficiently open-ended and neutral to allow their continuing adjustment, through interpretation, to changing societal conditions and demands.

The alternative approach – and it is a genuine alternative – is to attempt to do nothing at all about the court or its interpretation processes. Simply change the substance of what is to be interpreted – namely, sections 91 and 92 of the BNA Act. Prime Minister Trudeau seemed to be inclining towards this reasoning. In defending the court's decisions on Saskatchewan's taxation of natural resources as a 'correct interpretation of the law,' he said: 'I am pointing out that it is not the prime minister taking that position. It was the Supreme Court of Canada stating what the law is. I have indicated that we are flexible in our approach to changing the law.'[7]

At the same time, a study was commissioned by the Quebec Minister of Inter-Governmental Affairs, Claude Morin, and undertaken by an officer of his ministry, Gilbert L'Ecuyer. The study concludes that it is the text itself of the constitution, and not the interpretation – 'on the whole, faithful and well-founded in law' – that is responsible for the ever-increasing centralization of powers in the hands of the federal government.[8] These views – civil law and Cartesian – perhaps place too much emphasis on abstract written texts and ignore the human element in their application in specific cases.

Even a precisely drafted, legally 'fool-proof,' constitutional text may quickly become out-of-date and burdensome. A more general, open-ended text, however, may remain workable over a long period. Yet it still remains possible to achieve short-range solutions that should put the regulation of federal-provincial conflicts over legislative powers beyond the Supreme Court's capacity to interfere. However, prior federal-provincial consensus must be reached as to the scope and direction of the new constitutional compromise involved, whether taxation of natural resources, communications, or any other subject.

A solution in terms of the redrafting and redefinition of the division of powers would likely, of necessity, be limited to a term of years before it needed further recasting and redefinition. Yet it would avoid any unnecessary tinkering with the Supreme Court or with the Senate or other federal institutions. Some of the provincial proposals in this regard – for example, the idle talk of 'representative' provincial judges – compromise the integrity of the court and reflect a complete misunderstanding of the court's proper rôle.

The First Ministers' conference adjourned with the understanding that the parties would study Trudeau's list of seven matters where accord might be reached on a new definition of powers. They agreed to report back to a resumed conference on 5–6 February 1979. The Prime Minister had originally seemed to have in mind an eventual 'package deal.' In return for federal concessions to the provinces in the seven areas the provinces would accept proposals dear to the Prime Minister's heart. These include 'patriation' of the constitution to Canada; adoption of an autonomous, self-operating amending formula for the BNA Act; and constitutional 'entrenchment' of a new Charter of Rights and Freedoms (possibly including action on language rights).

The original draft communiqué of the conference, prepared by federal officials alone, running to eleven pages and comprising eleven sections, had covered these points. Several premiers, including Davis and Hatfield, would apparently have been prepared to go along with this. It was rejected by Lougheed and Lévesque because it went well beyond the short list discussed the day before, and simply amounted to a re-statement of federal government objectives alone. Lougheed and Lévesque made it clear that they would not agree to 'patriation' and to a new amending formula until agreement should be reached on the federal government's granting more legislative powers to the provinces.

The draft communiqué thus had to be replaced by a new vaguely worded one of two pages. Prime Minister Trudeau said, however, that he had not abandoned his original idea of a 1 July 1979 deadline for certain constitutional changes on the initiative of the federal government. He indicated that the federal government would not introduce any new constitutional legislation until after the February 1979 resumed conference.

The constitutional dialogue had thus been entered upon, even if it remained somewhat artificial and constrained. It is limited to the federal government and the provincial premiers. There has been neither direct popular consultation nor the presence of other participants in the Canadian political process such as municipal governments.

The ordering principles for any new consensus on constitutional change remain clear. *Federalism* is crucial: central government application of the equalization principle and the sharing, on a nation-wide basis, of the benefits and riches of the federal polity. *Dualism* must survive, in the recognition – formally, through informal 'glosses' on the constitution, or through *ad hoc* federal-provincial arrangements – of the special cultural and linguistic character of Quebec within Confederation. *Regionalism* is the third element: decentralization or devolution of decision-making power from the federal government to all of the provinces on an equal basis.

In many senses, however, these principles are in conflict: constitutional dualism is certainly not the same thing as constitutional regionalism. While the imperatives of the two may sometimes coincide or overlap, they will normally lead to quite different constitutional and institutional consequences[9] and therefore should not be confused. And federalism must recognize, honestly and openly, the extreme disparities presently existing in wealth and social and economic opportunity between the different provinces and seek to correct those disparities. Yet it must inevitably, at some point, take issue with the more extreme demands for local autonomy and regionalism. This is particularly so where the demands are simply directed to the self-interest of English-speaking premiers.

There is, indeed, a growing note of sadness entering into public appraisals of the performance of the main participants in the Confederation debate and their often parochial-claims. These are all too often advanced in the name of constitutional reform. Thus, it is recorded that in the debate in the Ontario legislature following the First Ministers' conference,

back benchers and opposition members are not nearly so concerned about gaining additional provincial power as the Davis Government and the other provincial premiers seem to be. In fact, speakers of all parties stressed the need for a strong central Government, and there were several disparaging remarks directed toward Alberta Premier Peter Lougheed for his claim that Prime Minister Pierre Trudeau does not speak for Canada ... Several speakers made it clear they see the national unity debate and the task of re-writing the constitution as a non-partisan affair. They want to have an opportunity to discuss and have an input into Ontario's *rôle* – but not to make partisan points.[10]

The same basic point was made by a West Coast editorialist in remarks addressed to Premier Bennett on the occasion of the publication of his new 'provinces-oriented' constitutional proposals:

What [Premier Bennett] cannot avoid, however, is the suspicion that he does not fully comprehend the federal system and that his proposed reforms are shamelessly parochial ... Confederation needs to be strengthened, not weakened. Especially now, with the country facing the twin strains of economic *malaise* and threatened Quebec separation ... Some changes and accommodations are necessary. That is obvious. But they need to be carefully thought out – not rushed as Mr. Trudeau originally wanted and not as ostensibly debasing to the federal concept as Mr. Bennett's proposals.[11]

Senator Eugene Forsey, referring to the same BC collection of constitutional 'reforms,' spoke wryly of 'provincial warlords ... mouthing this nonsense.'[12]

What has been gained is a large amount of pragmatism and reasonableness in the public constitutional dialogue before the television cameras and the reporters. The more experienced premiers – Lougheed, Blakeney, Hatfield, Davis, and not least Lévesque – know how gracefully to jettison rhetorical or overly abstract positions worked out in advance by academic consultants or civil servants. What emerges is a large element of political realism and ultimately, perhaps, of statesmanship. Premier Lévesque has moved noticeably, since the first flush of victory in 1976, from a separatist position to the request for a 'mandate for negotiation.'[13] The promised Quebec referendum has been postponed or delayed. Meanwhile, the federal position *vis-à-vis* Quebec becomes more flexible all the time, as reflected in a host of practical accommodations or arrangements between the two governments.[14]

This is, in essence, the dialectical development of constitutional law, based on intellectual debate and exchange, and reciprocal give-and-take in practical negotiations. It includes the possibility – the prime lesson from the Cuban Missile crisis – of allowing one's opponent to retreat from untenable positions without intolerable loss of face. For Quebec, such positions might conceivably include prior electoral commitments to separation from Canada. The federal and provincial governments should certainly avoid placing political or psychological barriers in the way of Quebec's retreating from such electoral commitments. In any event, in today's much more pragmatic federal policies towards Quebec, we can see a new, more pluralist approach to federalism – perhaps a renewed exercise in that older, Pearson conception of cooperative federalism.

The delayed Pépin-Robarts Commission Report, *A Future Together*, was released on 25 January 1979. In its most striking passage, the report asks the rhetorical question, 'Does Quebec possess the right of self-determination?' and concludes 'if, in the course of the next few years, Quebecers decided, definitively and democratically, to secede,' then the answer should be 'an unequivocal yes,' as 'a virtual corollary of our acceptance of the democratic process.' This is to dare to speak the politically unspeakable, and is in keeping with the courage, intellectual honesty, and generosity of outlook with which the commission approached its task.

The report also recognizes Quebec's 'unique position' based on its 'distinctive culture and heritage,' and though specifically rejecting 'special constitutional status,' seems to embrace it on an informal basis when it recommends that all the provinces should be allotted powers 'in the areas needed by Quebec ... but ... in a manner which would enable the other provinces, if they so wished, not to exercise these responsibilities and instead leave them to Ottawa.'

The commission opts clearly for provincial protection and determination of the scope of language rights within any province, and also has some not unfavourable words for Quebec's Bill 101.

The commission also makes detailed recommendations for a substantial decentralization of the Canadian federal system in the name of 'regionalism.' This part of the commission's work seems more questionable and open to technical and political criticisms. The commission perhaps succumbs too easily to the 'numbers' game: the Supreme Court is to jump from nine to eleven judges; a new federal upper house is to have sixty members; there are to be sixty new members elected at large for the federal lower house. There is an ironic contrast between the archaic notion of appointed delegations from the provinces to the upper house and the modern idea of proportional representation to be applied in the lower house.

These recommendations on Parliament and the Supreme Court are quite categorical but not well researched or considered. They do not always seem self-consistent or necessarily to flow from the stated assumptions. Taken as a whole, they suggest that the commission members may have put them all together and decided to let history resolve any contradictions!

In spite of the report's insistence that its recommendations 'represent an integrated set of proposals linked to each other' and should not be considered separately, they can be viewed as a range of models available for the negotiations that will certainly follow in the next few years. The continuing dialectic will undoubtedly advance to new ground as a result of the more consciously pluralistic emphasis given to the constitutional debate by the publication of the commission's report.

Notes

NOTES TO INTRODUCTION

1 Paul Weiler *The Province* Vancouver 9 Mar. 1978
2 See François Cloutier *L'enjeu. Mémoires politiques 1970–1976* (1978) pp. 13
   et seq.; though note the prophetic editorial by Tom Symons *J. Can. Stud.*
   (May 1970) 1
3 Quoted by Geoffrey Stevens *Globe and Mail* Toronto 4 Mar. 1978

NOTES TO CHAPTER ONE

1 This part of the discussion draws upon the author's *Federal Constitution-Making
   for a Multi-National World* (1966), and *Comparative Federalism. States' Rights and
   National Power* (2nd ed 1965). See also R.R. Bowie and Carl J. Friedrich eds
   Studies in Federalism (1954); A.W. Macmahon ed *Federalism. Mature and
   Emergent* (1955)
2 Dicey *Introduction to the Study of the Law of the Constitution* (1st ed 1885; 9th ed
   1939) ed E.C.S. Wade pp. 171–5
3 Dicey *England's case against Home Rule* (1886); H.J. Laski *Parliamentary Government in England* (1948) p. 344
4 Compare Léon Dion *Le Devoir* Montreal 19 Nov. 1977

NOTES TO CHAPTER TWO

1 The discussion on judicial review of the constitution draws generally upon the
   author's *Judicial Review in the English-Speaking World* (4th ed 1969); *Comparative
   Federalism, States' Rights and National Power* (2nd ed 1965) chap. 3 pp. 21 et seq.;
   Constitutionalism in Germany and the Federal Constitutional Court (1962)

2 1 Cranch 137, 2 L. Ed. 60 (1803)
3 30 & 31 Vict., c. 3 (1867)
4 Vincent C. MacDonald 'The Constitution in a Changing World' 26 *Can. Bar Rev.* 21 (1948)
5 *Attorney-General for Ontario* v. *Attorney-General for Canada* [1912] A.C. 571, 581 (P.C.)
6 W.P.M. Kennedy 'The Interpretation of the British North America Act' 8 *Camb. Law J.* 146, 150 (1942)
7 See, in particular, *Russell* v. *The Queen* (1882) 7 App. Cas. 829, 839 (1882)
8 *Attorney-General for Ontario* v. *Attorney-General for Canada* [1896] A.C. 348 (P.C.) per Lord Watson; and see also his decision in *Tennant* v. *Union Bank* [1894] A.C. 31 (P.C.)
9 *In re Board of Commerce Act* [1922] 1 A.C. 191 (P.C.); *Toronto Electric Commissioners* v. *Snider* [1925] A.C. 396 (P.C.)
10 *Attorney-General for Canada* v. *Attorney-General for Ontario* [1937] A.C. 326 (P.C.) per Lord Atkin, especially 350. See Lord Wright in 33 *Can. Bar Rev.* 1123 (1955); F.R. Scott 34 *Can. Bar Rev.* 114 (1956); B.J. MacKinnon ibid. 115; and the author ibid. 243
11 *The King* v. *Eastern Terminal Elevator Co.* [1925] S.C.R. 434, 442
12 *Edwards* v. *Attorney-General for Canada* [1930] A.C. 124, 136 (P.C.)
13 [1935] A.C. 500, 518 (P.C.)
14 *Attorney-General for Ontario* v. *Attorney-General for Canada* [1947] A.C. 127, 154 (P.C.) (Reference re Privy Council Appeals) per Lord Jowitt
15 MacDonald 'The Constitution' 21, 44
16 W.P.M. Kennedy 'The Constitution of Canada' 2 *Politica* 356 (1937)
17 Kennedy *The Constitution of Canada* (2nd ed 1938) p. 550
18 Bora Laskin ' "Peace, Order and Good Government" Reexamined' 25 *Can. Bar Rev.* 1054, 1086 (1947)
19 Lord Haldane 'The Judicial Committee of the Privy Council' 1 *Camb. Law J.* 143, 150 (1923)
20 7 App. Cas. 829 (1882)
21 Kennedy *Constitution* p. 431
22 See Louis-Philippe Pigeon 'The Meaning of Provincial Autonomy' 29 *Can. Bar Rev.* 1126, 1134 (1951)
23 *Toronto Electric Commissioners* v. *Snider* [1925] A.C. 396 (P.C.)
24 MacDonald 'The Constitution' 44
25 Kennedy *Constitution* p. 550
26 *In re Natural Products Marketing Act* [1936] S.C.R. 398
27 *In re Board of Commerce Act* [1920] 60 S.C.R. 456

28 Bora Laskin '"Peace, Order and Good Government"' 1054, 1056; and see also Laskin 'The Supreme Court of Canada: A Final Court of and for Canadians' 29 *Can. Bar Rev.* 1038, 1057 et seq. (1951)

29 See, for example, *Roncarelli* v. *Duplessis* 16 D.L.R. (2d) 689 (1959); and see the author's analysis in 37 *Can. Bar Rev.* 503 (1959)

30 *Reference re Ownership of Off-Shore Mineral Rights* 65 D.L.R. (2d) 353 (1968). And see the analysis by Hubbard 'Constitutional Law: International Law: Ownership of and Jurisdiction over Off-shore Mineral Rights' 2 *Ott. Law Rev.* 212 (1967); and by the author, in 2 *La Rev. Jur. Thém.* (Université de Montréal) 277, 279 (1967–8)

NOTES TO CHAPTER THREE

1 Jacques-Yvan Morin 'Le fédéralisme canadien après cent ans' 2 *Rev. jur. Thém.* 13, 14 (1967–8)

2 J.-Y. Morin 'Vers un nouvel équilibre constitutionnel au Canada' in C.B. Macpherson and P.-A. Crépeau eds *The Future of Canadian Federalism* (1965) pp. 141 et seq.

3 Ibid. pp. 142 et seq.; J.-Y. Morin 'Le fédéralisme' 19 et seq.

4 J.-Y. Morin 'Un équilibre' 143

5 J.-Y. Morin 'Le fédéralisme' 24

6 J.-Y. Morin 'Les origines historiques du statut particulier' 20 *Rev. d'hist. de l'am. fr.* 3–5 (1966)

7 J.-Y. Morin 'Le Québec et l'arbitrage constitutionnel: de Charybde en Scylla' 45 *Can. Bar Rev.* 608 (1967)

8 Claude Morin *Le pouvoir québécois en négociation* (1972) pp. 71 et seq.

9 Ibid. p. 136

10 Ibid. p. 137

11 Ibid. p. 153

12 Pigeon 'Provincial Autonomy' 1126, 1135

13 Marcel Faribault *Vers une nouvelle constitution* (1967); Faribault *La Révision constitutionnelle* (1970); Faribault and Robert M. Fowler *Ten to One: The Confederation Wager* (1965)

14 Daniel Johnson *Brief on the Constitution, Government of Quebec* p. 7. Presented to the Canadian Inter-governmental Conference, Ottawa, 5–7 Feb. 1968

15 Ibid. p. 29

16 Guy Saint-Pierre *La réforme des institutions politiques québécoises* (June 1975) pp. 2 et seq., 25 et seq., 323 et seq.

17 Jacques Brossard, André Patry, and Elisabeth Weiser *Les Pouvoirs extérieurs du Québec* (1967)
18 Jacques Brossard *La Cour suprême et la Constitution. Le forum constitutionnel au Canada* (1968)
19 Jacques Brossard *L'accession à la souveraineté et le cas du Québec* (1976). See also Brossard 'Le droit du peuple québécois de disposer de lui-même au regard du droit international' 15 *Can. Yrbk. of Int. Law* 84 (1977)
20 Brossard *L'accession* pp. 311 et seq.
21 Gérard Bergeron *L'indépendance: Oui, mais ...* (1977) pp. 163 et seq.
22 Gérald Beaudoin *Le Devoir* 20 and 22 Aug. 1977 and 12 June 1978
23 André Tremblay *Le Devoir* 28 and 29 Oct. 1977
24 Gérard Bergeron *Le Devoir* 20 Jan. 1978
25 Cloutier *L'enjeu* pp. 13 et seq.
26 Claude Ryan 'Réflexions sur les défis des prochaines décennies' *Le Devoir* 4 and 5 Apr. 1978
27 *Protestant School Board of Greater Montreal* v. *Minister of Education of the Province of Quebec et al.* Superior Court, Montreal, judgment of 6 Apr. 1976, [1976] C.S. 430; 83 D.L.R. (3d) 645 (1978); *Blaikie et al.* c. *Procureur-général de la Province de Québec et Procureur-général du Canada* Superior Court, Montreal, judgment of 23 Jan. 1978, 85 D.L.R. (3d) 252 (1978)

NOTES TO CHAPTER FOUR

1 *Attorney-General for Canada* v. *Attorney-General for Ontario* [1937] A.C. 326 (P.C.) per Lord Atkin
2 [1936] S.C.R. 461
3 See the statement by Paul Gérin-Lajoie *Montreal Star* 19 Mar. 1968
4 See 'Franco-Canadian Cultural Agreement' 17 *External Affairs* (Ottawa) 513 (Dec. 1965); 'Text of Cultural Agreement between the Government of Canada and the Government of the French Republic' ibid. 514; 'Entente on Cultural Cooperation between France and Quebec' ibid. 520; 'Text of Entente on Cultural Cooperation between the Government of the French Republic and the Government of Quebec' ibid. 521
5 65 D.L.R. (2d) 376 (1968)
6 Ibid. 380
7 *In re Regulation and Control of Aeronautics* [1932] A.C. 54 (P.C.)
8 *Johannesson* v. *The Rural Municipality of West St. Paul* [1952] S.C.R. 292
9 *Attorney-General for Canada* v. *Attorney-General for Ontario* [1937] A.C. 326, 354 (P.C.) (*Labour Conventions* case) per Lord Atkin

NOTES TO CHAPTER FIVE

1 See 'Extraits inédits d'un journal intime: André Laurendeau, La longue marche vers l'égalité' *Le Devoir* 1 June 1978; Michel Roy 'André Laurendeau: 10 ans plus tard' *Le Devoir* 1 June 1978
2 Guy Favreau *White Paper: The Amendment of the Constitution of Canada* (1965)
3 Official Languages Act 1968–9 c. 54
4 *Jones* v. *Attorney-General of Canada et al.* 45 D.L.R. (3d) 583 (1974)
5 The Special Joint Committee of the Senate and of the House of Commons on the Constitution of Canada *Final Report* (4th Sess., 28th Parl. 1972). For Quebec critiques, see Laurent Laplante 'Un rapport stimulant mais centralisateur' *Le Devoir* 20 Mar. 1972; Claude Ryan 'Le comité Molgat-MacGuigan et le pouvoir de dépenser d'Ottawa' *Le Devoir* 22 Mar. 1972
6 *Reference re Ownership of Off-Shore Mineral Rights* 65 D.L.R. (2d) 353 (1968)
7 *Attorney-General for Canada* v. *Attorney-General for Ontario* [1937] A.C. 326 (P.C.)
8 'Deux dissidences' *Le Devoir* 17 Mar. 1972; Claude Lemelin *Le Devoir* 20 Mar. 1972; Jean-Pierre Bonhomme *Le Devoir* 18 Mar. 1972

NOTES TO CHAPTER SIX

1 *Rapport de la Commission d'enquête sur la situation de la langue française et sur les droits linguistiques au Québec* vol 2 *Les droits linguistiques* (1972) p. 10
2 *Rapport de la Commission d'enquête* vol 1 *La langue de travail*; vol 2 *Les droits linguistiques*; vol 3 *Les groupes ethniques*
3 *Rapport* vol 2 pp. 65 et seq. and 78–80
4 Ibid. pp. 79
5 Loi sur la langue officielle (Bill 22, National Assembly, assented to 31 July 1974)
6 See Cloutier *L'enjeu* pp. 84–5
7 Loi pour promouvoir la langue française au Québec (Bill 63, National Assembly, assented to 28 Nov. 1969). And see Cloutier *L'enjeu* pp. 78–9; Cloutier *L'avenir de la langue française au Québec* (1971); Cloutier *La loi sur la langue officielle au Québec (Bill 22)* (1974)
8 Cloutier *L'enjeu* pp. 77 et seq., and especially 85–7
9 'Fredericton demande que la loi passe le test de la Cour suprême' *Le Devoir* 10 Aug. 1974; 'Lettre de M. Trudeau á M. Hatfield' *Le Devoir* 16 Sept. 1974; 'Le Bill 22: Richard Hatfield a manqué à la courtoisie fédérale' *Le Devoir* 5 Oct. 1974
10 *Protestant School Board of Greater Montreal* v. *Minister of Education of the Province of Quebec et al.* Superior Court, Montreal, judgment of 6 Apr. 1976, [1976] C.S. 430; 83 D.L.R. (3d) 645 (1978)

11 *Trustees of the Roman Catholic Separate Schools for the City of Ottawa* v. *Mackell* [1917] A.C. 62, 74 (P.C.)

12 *Thorson* v. *Attorney-General of Canada et al. (no. 2)* 43 D.L.R. (3d) 1 (1974)

13 *Nova Scotia Board of Censors* v. *McNeil* 55 D.L.R. (3d) 632 (1975)

14 *Livre Blanc: La politique québécoise de la langue française* (1977)

15 Charte de la langue française au Québec (National Assembly, assented to 26 Aug. 1977)

16 See Cloutier *L'enjeu* p. 87

17 'Upstaging Pierre' *The Province* 25 July 1977

18 William Davis 'Une affaire de principe, non de négociations bilatérales' *Le Devoir* 1 Aug. 1977

19 Ryan 'L'impossible projet de M. Trudeau' *Le Devoir* 12 Sept. 1977

20 *Campisi et al.* c. *Procureur-général de la Province de Québec et al.* Superior Court, Montreal, judgment of 19 Dec. 1977

21 *Protestant School Board of Greater Montreal* v. *Minister of Education of the Province of Quebec et al.* Superior Court, Montreal, judgment of 6 Apr. 1976, [1976] C.S. 430; 83 D.L.R. (3d) 645 (1978)

22 *Blaikie et al.* c. *Procureur-général de la Province de Québec et Procureur-général du Canada* Superior Court, Montreal, judgment of 23 Jan. 1978, 85 D.L.R. (3d) 252 (1978)

23 Cloutier *L'enjeu* pp. 91–2

24 'Les articles 93 et 133' *Le Devoir* 14 Mar. 1978

25 'La Charte québécoise du français: Ottawa trouve que la loi 101 est mauvaise mais préfère le recours régulier aux tribunaux' (press statement issued by federal government 6 Oct. 1977) *Le Devoir* 7 Oct. 1977

NOTES TO CHAPTER SEVEN

1 Government of Ontario, Ontario Advisory Committee on Confederation *The Confederation Challenge. Background Papers and Reports* vol 1 (1967), vol 2 (1970)

2 Government of Ontario *First Report of the Advisory Committee on Confederation* (1978) pp. 2–11, 18. For a Quebec appraisal of the Davis committee, see Claude Turcotte *Le Devoir* 3 July 1978

3 Progressive Conservative party *Discussion Paper, The Constitution and National Unity* (1978)

4 W.R. Bennett *What is British Columbia's position on the Constitution of Canada?* (1976)

5 W.R. Bennett *A brief presented to the Task Force on National Unity* (1978) pp. 9, 11

6 *Report of the Western Premiers' Task Force on Constitutional Trends* (1977) pp. 36, 42–3, 50–1
7 80 D.L.R. (3d) 449 (1978)
8 79 D.L.R. (3d) 203 (1978) (Saskatchewan Court of Appeal)
9 *Report of the Western Premiers' Task Force* p. 50
10 *Second Report of the Western Premiers' Task Force* (1978) p. 30
11 *A Summary Report on the Proceedings of 'Alternatives Canada', a Canada West Conference on Confederation held at Banff, March 27–29, 1978* (1978)
12 D. Elton, F.C. Engelman, and P. McCormick *Discussion Paper, Alternatives: Towards the development of an effective federal system for Canada* for Canada West Foundation (1978)
13 Editorial *Globe* 1 Apr. 1978; editorial *Le Devoir* 1 Apr. 1978
14 Government of Alberta *Position Paper on Constitutional Change, Harmony in Diversity: a new Federalism for Canada* (1978)

NOTES TO CHAPTER EIGHT

1 [1922] 1 A.C. 191 (P.C.), see also *Toronto Electric Commissioners v. Snider* [1925] A.C. 396 (P.C.)
2 *Reference re Anti-Inflation Act* 68 D.L.R. (3d) 452 (1976)
3 Ibid. 498
4 Ibid.
5 Ibid. 494
6 Ibid. 506 et seq.
7 'Address to the Seminar for Journalists, Ottawa, February 22, 1978'
8 A reference apparently to Edwin R. Black 'Supreme Court judges as spear-carriers for Ottawa: "They need watching"' *Report on Confederation* Feb. 1978 12
9 *In re Regulation and Control of Radio Communications* [1932] A.C. 304 (P.C.)
10 [1932] A.C. 54 (P.C.)
11 [1937] A.C. 326 (P.C.)
12 *Re Public Service Board et al., Dionne et al., and Attorney-General of Canada et al.* 83 D.L.R. (3d) 178 (1978)
13 Ibid. 181
14 81 D.L.R. (3d) 609 (1978)
15 Ibid. 621
16 *Canadian Industrial Gas and Oil Ltd v. Government of Saskatchewan et al.* 80 D.L.R. (3d) 449 (1978)
17 Peter Mosher *Globe* 1 Nov. 1978
18 Geoffrey Stevens *Globe* 2 Nov. 1978

19 76 D.L.R. (3d) 455 (1977) (Federal Court, Trial Division)
20 22 N.R. 328 (1978) (Federal Court of Appeal)

NOTES TO CHAPTER NINE

1 See Michel Roy *Le Devoir* 13 June 1978; and Lise Bissonnette *Le Devoir* 10 June 1978
2 See *White Paper, The Canadian Constitution and Constitutional Amendment* and *Highlights* (1978)

NOTES TO CHAPTER TEN

1 'La déclaration de Regina' *Le Devoir* 12 Aug. 1978; *Vancouver Sun* 12 Aug. 1978

NOTES TO CHAPTER ELEVEN

1 Senate, Special Committee of the Senate on the Constitution *First Report* 10 Oct. 1978
2 Senate, House of Commons, Special Joint Committee on the Constitution of Canada *Report to Parliament* 10 Oct. 1978
3 *Discussion Paper, Alternatives* pp. 13–21
4 See Senate, House of Commons *Minutes of Joint Committee on the Constitution* (1978) pp. 11–14; and Canada West Foundation *A Summary Report on the Proceedings of the Colloquia on Constitutional Change August 28–31, 1978* (1978)

NOTES TO CHAPTER TWELVE

1 'Ryan: le projet Trudeau' and Michel Roy *Le Devoir* 13 July 1978
2 Richard Joy *Les minorités des langues officielles au Canada* (1978); P. des Rivières 'Le Canada paraît se diriger vers deux unilinguismes' *Le Devoir* 7 Sept. 1978
3 Joy *Les Minorités*
4 Articles by Léon Dion, Claude Turcotte *Le Devoir* 21 Sept. 1978
5 J.V. Clyne 'The Constitution of Canada. A Summing Up' (Address to the Vancouver Institute, given 11 Feb. 1978) published in *The Province* 18 Mar. 1978; and see also J.V. Clyne 'The national will and the constitution' *Vancouver Sun* 21 July 1978
6 Anthony Westell *The New Society* (1977) pp. 55 et seq.

NOTES TO CHAPTER THIRTEEN

1 Michel Roy *Le Devoir* 30 Oct. 1978
2 Jeffrey Simpson *Globe* 26 and 31 Oct. 1978
3 See 'Déclaration de M. René Lévesque' *Le Devoir* 31 Oct. 1978
4 Geoffrey Stevens *Globe* 2 Nov. 1978
5 Hugh Winsor *Globe* 1 Nov. 1978
6 'A carrot to dangle before the provincial donkeys' *The Province* 17 Oct. 1978
7 'Ottawa grant tax eyed on natural resources' *Vancouver Sun* 21 Oct. 1978
8 Jean-Claude Picard *Le Devoir* 18 Oct. 1978
9 'Le Québec devrait bénéficier' *Le Devoir* 30 Oct. 1978
10 Hugh Winsor 'Strands of concern and regret' *Globe* 9 Nov. 1978; see also Gérard Bergeron *Le Devoir* 11 Nov. 1978
11 'Put Canada First' *Vancouver Sun* 19 Oct. 1978
12 'Umpire is out' Letter to the Editor *Globe* 11 Nov. 1978
13 See the declarations made by Premier Lévesque on 11 Oct. 1978: 'Par référendum' *Le Devoir* 13 Oct. 1978
14 See, for example, Ian Rodger *Globe* 16 Nov. 1978

Index

Also by the same author:

Judicial Review (1956; 4th ed 1969)
Föderalismus und Bundesverfassungsrecht (1962)
Constitutionalism in Germany (1962)
Comparative Federalism (1962; 2nd ed 1965)
'Peaceful Coexistence' and Soviet-Western International Law (1964)
Federal Constitution-Making for a Multi-National World (1966)
International Law and World Revolution (1967)
Conflit idéologique et Ordre public mondial (1970)
with Jean-Denis Gendron et al. *La Situation de la langue française au Québec*
    3 vols (1973)
The Illegal Diversion of Aircraft and International Law (1975)
Parliamentary Privilege and the Publication of Parliamentary Debates (1975)
*The International Law of Détente. Arms Control, European Security, and East-West
    Cooperation* (1978)
The World Court and the International Law-Making Process (1978)

Editor of:

Canadian Jurisprudence. The Civil Law and Common Law in Canada (1958)
Law, Foreign Policy, and the East-West Détente (1964)
with M.A. Bradley *The Freedom of the Air* (1968)
with M.A. Bradley *New Frontiers in Space Law* (1969)
The International Law of Communications (1970)
Aerial Piracy and International Law (1971)
with P. Pescatore *Federalism and Supreme Courts and the Integration of Legal Systems*
    (1973)